RIGHT BRAIN/LEFT BRAIN
PHOTOGRAPHY

RIGHT BRAIN/ LEFT BRAIN PHOTOGRAPHY

KATHRYN MARX

AMPHOTO

AN IMPRINT OF WATSON-GUPTILL
PUBLICATIONS/NEW YORK

Kathryn Marx has been living in Paris and New York for the past 10 years. Her photography is part of international public and private collections, including those of the Carnavalet Museum, Paris; Marjorie and Leonard Vernon, California; the Nicéphore Niepce Museum, Chalon Sur Saône; Shearson Lehman, New York; the Maison Européène, Paris; the New York Public Library; and the Bibliothèque Nationale, Paris. Thanks to a generous grant from Eastman Kodak, Marx is currently building photographic mobiles.

HALF-TITLE PAGE:
THE COLLAR © RALPH GIBSON.

TITLE PAGE:
© FRANCO FONTANA.

DEDICATION PAGE:
© KATHRYN MARX.

CONTENTS PAGE:
SPILL. © JIM GOLDSMITH.

Editorial concept by Robin Simmen
Edited by Liz Harvey
Designed by Areta Buk
Graphic production by Ellen Greene

Copyright © 1994 by Kathryn Marx
First published 1994 in New York by Amphoto,
an imprint of Watson-Guptill Publications,
a division of BPI Communications, L.P.,
1515 Broadway, New York, NY 10036

Library of Congress Cataloging-in-Publication Data

Marx, Kathryn.
 Right brain/left brain photography : the art and technique of 70 modern masters / by Kathryn Marx.
 Includes index.
 ISBN 0-8174-5717-8
 1. Photography, Artistic. 2. Photographers—Interviews.
 3. Aesthetics. 4. Cerebral dominance. I. Title.
 TR642.M364 1994
 770—dc20   93-43031
                                                     CIP

Manufactured in Italy

1 2 3 4 5 6 7 8 9/01 00 99 98 97 96 95 94

My gratitude to the following people for their unflinching support:

Liz Harvey, Robin Simmen, and Jason Schneider, for their confidence from the right-brain beginnings of this book's creation; Julia Van Haaften; Louise Adler; Gigi Saada; Susan Fletcher; Patrick Boucher; Annich Lucchini; Kazé Kuromochi; Valerie Servant; Marjorie and Leonard Vernon; Evelynne Daitz; Jean Pierre Lambert; Christian Bouqueret; Ann Marie Gourbeault; Maggie Brenner; Marie Claude Lebon; Xavier Roux; Jacqueline Schmitt; Simon Edwards; Romy Baron; Dr. Gregory Fried; Ruth Morrison; Nancy Wilson Pajíc; Margie Lefcourt; John Alden Drury; Gail T. Bressler; Nicola Sheara; my parents, Emilie and Arthur Marx, for giving me my healthy left and right brain to begin with; my brothers, Alfred and Arthur; Ann Rodiger, for helping me see further; and Patricia Ann Mullen, for opening my third eye.

 I would also like to thank the participating photographers for their generous contributions to the world of their art— and to this book.

DEDICATED TO THE MEMORY OF AARON SISKIND

CONTENTS

PREFACE

WHAT PROMPTED MY INTEREST in the difference between right-brain and left-brain photography was seeing two photographs of the same place that reflected two completely different approaches to the subject, both of which the artist considered to be equally representative of the location. I recognized that the impulses for the two photographic perspectives came from two different "places" within the artist.

The first signal that I might be on to something occurred after I read Betty Edwards's book, *Drawing on the Right Side of the Brain*. I realized that photographing is a more direct expression of an impulse than drawing is. The reason is simple: In photography, the eye's response need not pass down to the hand and pause there in order for the photographer to register an image on paper.

Instead, the impulse passes from the eye to the fingertip on the shutter-release button while the eye remains fixed on the subject.

How much more spontaneous can artists be than to register at once what their eye perceives? Addressing this point, I arrived at two different answers. One kind of photograph requires artists to pass impulses through the filter of their intellect. This way, the realized image has been digested and directed to correspond to the artists' intentions. This kind of photograph is taken to show, explain, or express something specific about the subject. Logic directs the process until the artists feel that their purpose has been successfully achieved. Another kind of photograph of the same subject bypasses any filter between the artists' eye and the end of

STOP. DEATH VALLEY. © ANGELO LOMEO.

their finger on the shutter-release button in order to capture the image intuitively. The first approach is well thought out; the second is a process guided by a purely intuitive sense of the subject.

I then decided that it would take a book to fully cover the subtle differences and similarities between these two contrasting approaches to consummating artistic desires. Some people are compelled to examine, explain, or justify the subjects of their photographs; these are left-brain photographers. Photographers who spontaneously dive into the shooting of a subject without forethought and fall in love at first sight are right-brain oriented.

I knew that I would be taking on quite a challenge if I were to start asking photographers to speak about their "unexplainable impulses," their moments of creativity. Clearly, photographers are photographers because they prefer this art form of nonverbal communication. However, I hoped at least that left-brain photographers whose work is based on an intellectual approach would provide verbal explanations a little more readily than their right-brain counterparts. But, surprisingly, this hasn't always been the case. A well-analyzed idea still includes moments of "blind" instinct. After all, a properly functioning brain is one whose right and left hemispheres work as a united whole. My own brain then concluded that it would be worthwhile to investigate photographic impulses in order to find out more about our potentials, God-given or learned, all derived from somewhere between the left and right hemispheres of our brains.

POND REFLECTION #2. © SONJA BULLATY.

INTRODUCTION

RIGHT UP FRONT, I want to make it clear that I'm not a scientist but a photographer. I've completed considerable research on the subject of right- and left-brain potentials in hopes of better understanding the inner workings of my photography as well as that of my colleagues. When I first read about drawing with the right brain, I wondered why no one had addressed the left- and right-brain aspects of photography. After all, the camera is one of the most direct means of expressing what happens between the brain and the eye.

Today the camera is the most sensitive of all the instruments that record what the human eye sees. Although the camera has become more and more sophisticated, the eye is still a little more advanced! But the camera is faster and much more direct than a hand holding a pencil to draw with. This is especially true of the new automated cameras. Pressing the shutter-release button to photograph an image in your mind's eye takes only a split second; manifesting impulses that pass from the brain down the arm and then to the hand takes much longer.

To capture the most accurate image of a subject, some left-brain photographers believe that it is imperative to have—and to master—all of the latest technology that the human brain's left hemisphere can comprehend and manage. This is the only way that their initial effort can lead to their artistic satisfaction. Yet some of the greatest photographers use the most basic Polaroid cameras, old Donald Duck cameras, or Instamatic cameras. For these right-brain photographers, the art is in the simplest recording of what they see and how they frame their subject. Neither approach is more or less creative; both enable photographers and viewers to enjoy the entire spectrum.

Corresponding to these two dimensions of expression are the left and right hemispheres of the brain, and, therefore, left- and right-brain-oriented photography as well. As such, left-brain-oriented pictures are more directed, previsualized, and literal than right-brain-oriented images. It follows, then, that right-brain photographs are more subjective and often more abstract photographs, catering to the photographer's point of view rather than to someone else's particular demands.

In regard to the images in this book, the terms "left brain" and "right brain" arise from the photographer's predominant state of mind at the time of the picture-taking. These labels aren't based on the side of the brain the images stimulate in viewers, nor are they meant to brand the photographers themselves. The terms "left brain" and "right brain" apply to the free-flowing stimuli behind photography's nonverbal communication, no matter how exact or unrecognizable the resulting image of the subject may be. The right brain stimulates the abstract realm of the photographer's mind; the left brain, on the other hand, directs the artist's expression of an explicit message.

Often, an abstract right-brain photograph is considered "artistic." However, after you read this book, you'll see that left-brain directives require as much "artistic" savoir-faire as right-brain commands do. Some photographers think that it is more difficult to follow the right brain's spontaneous impulses than to take a concrete approach with the left brain via an objective analysis. Other photographers find it is easier not to think at all, but to "feel the subject."

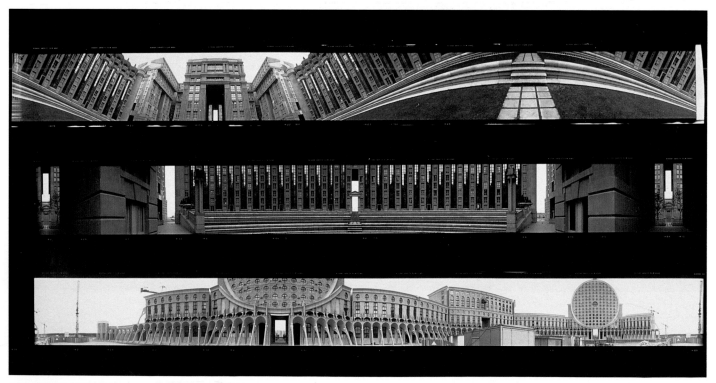

© DOMINIQUE GAESSLER.

10

HOLLAND CLOUDS AND SHADOW. © PETE TURNER.

PHOTOGRAPHERS' DESCRIPTIONS of the shooting process often contain some clear-cut clues that indicate that the right brain had the upper hand. For example, the word "instinctual" clearly and succinctly signifies that the photographer's right brain was at work, and the phrase "that moment or never" suggests profound spontaneity. The right brain governs the impulses that most people explain as an "unexplainable" reaction to a "particular moment." As Pete Turner reveals, his right-brain impulses guided the creation of a picture of clouds (above).

> This photograph was taken instinctively. This is what I am most interested in, and this is the most fun you can have. It is a decisive moment not oriented to anything. It is a natural thing at a peak at a certain time, like the light in this image and the clouds. It was that moment or never that the shot had to be taken. You just feel it is good. It is the beauty of what we do as photographers. You just sense it. At a certain point in your life or in your career, you know if it is right or not.

જ્જ

ARTISTS HAVE THEIR OWN "natural reaction" to subjects, which inspire their "particular moment" of right-brain creativity, whether this manifests itself in words, photographs, paintings, or any other form of expression. When the finished artwork conveys something to viewers, the creative moment is considered to be successful— whether they like the result or not. Because culture often strongly influences viewers, they may not appreciate variations of creativity until "culture" catches up to the artist and deems the work valuable.

Turner's sense of fun, which mystics believe is part of an individual's most enlightened self, is evident in this photograph as well. The next time you are in the midst of having fun, stop and ask yourself what you've been thinking about while having such a good time. The chances will be very good that you won't have been thinking at all; you'll simply have been yourself, or you'll have been completely immersed in the activity. Although the mind puts your thoughts in motion, the mind's left-brain thinking process can also get in between your actions and your impulses. The best advice anyone could give artists is to have "fun" with their "work." For another shot, Turner worked with an optical printer and manipulated two photographs together (opposite). As his description of the process shows, the merging of the images was carefully thought out.

I put together two different photographs. I felt the tulips were like pointillism, dots of color. As the foreground had this quality, I then added the photograph of the galaxy. It was like playing with a child's coloring set.

☙

TURNER IS STILL PLAYING HERE, but this is another form of play. In this case, he put pieces together, which is the convergent function of the left brain. The result is a fit, but it might not correspond to a combination that you find logical or rational. Summoning its own private logic, Turner's left brain directed his deduction that the two images worked together well this way.

This impulse isn't the same kind of impulse that drives a photographer to spontaneously take a single divergent or separate picture within one particular split second. You can look at a group of individual images and take seconds, minutes, hours, or years to decide how you ultimately want to arrange them. Regardless of the length of time, the left brain's tendency to integrate is essential.

STARRY NIGHT, 1990.
© PETE TURNER.

MAKING CHOICES

THE MOMENT THAT PHOTOGRAPHERS put their eye to the camera's viewfinder, endless possibilities and choices immediately appear in the frame of the lens. These external variables trigger the photographers' shutter-release finger, even when the photographers already have an image in mind. The previsualized image often responds to unexpected, on-the-spot conditions. There is no escaping the present.

Incorporating the unforeseen with the foreseen is a right-brain function. But the freedom to listen to your intuition isn't always available upon command. In most people's daily lives, intuition often isn't cultivated or encouraged. In fact, for the most part it is squelched in favor of following the dictums of the workplace. People's minds are filled with concepts and previsualized ideas, some of which they are consciously aware of and others that take them by surprise.

As a photographer, amateur or professional, you owe it to yourself and to your art to take full advantage of your right-brain intuition. So freely pick and choose from all the options you have, and impulsively pursue the cropping, angles, techniques, and

UNTITLED NYC, 1992. C-PRINT, 20 × 24". © MARIA MATTHEWS.

absence of techniques that make you happiest with your results. If you feel uncomfortable with the idea of accepting your instincts and fulfilling an innate desire to have fun, keep in mind that the founders of the United States felt the need to confirm the right to pursue happiness in the Declaration of Independence.

As you shoot, you'll discover that there is an infinite number of potential shots above, below, and around you. In addition to choosing among all of these possible pictures, you must decide whether to interpret your surroundings with left-brain literalness or right-brain subjectivity. Should you put the images together, leave them as individual fragments, or combine them in a series? Maria Matthews arranged the following images in various combinations (below left).

I lifted three images from contexts unbeknownst to the others for placement in this piece. I measured and set their scale, determined their visibility, added the fourth element of a three-dimensional object, visualized the image boundaries mandated by the camera, and shifted the elements to all fit within a white frame, and with the camera I kidnapped these visual references and locked them into a frame. Now, together, their meaning is legible in a way never before possible. I call it a fiction as I call all images. I invite you to enjoy the story of the man, the boy, and the etched image behind (of men in an English prison during a century gone by).

かか

RATHER THAN PUTTING PIECES TOGETHER with the help of the left brain, Denis Charmion made a single photograph, which most people would label a fragment of a scene (opposite). This picture was the result of an impulse; the photographer gave no thought to its meaning or message. Upon viewing the resulting image, Charmion was able to explain the reasoning that went on behind his eye while he pressed the shutter-release button. But at that moment, the experience was nonverbal.

The way that I took this photograph, I couldn't have taken any other way, and yet it is very hard to explain why. I found the form of the square very strong, as well as the primary color yellow. When I examine the photograph now, I see that if I had photographed the second lamp as well, I would have simply had two squares. Instead, the lamps made the squares look repetitive by going in the opposite direction. It seems that the lamps break the rhythm and yet bring another rhythm and another dimension. It was the lamps punctuating the repetition of the geometrical shapes which caught my eye. But when I took the picture, I wasn't thinking of any of this at all.

かか

REMEMBER, THE LEFT BRAIN is deductive, logical, and rationally directed to be concrete and analytically explicit. With its objectivity and sequential talents, it possesses an intellectual sense of convergence. The eye guided most strongly by the left brain is the one famous for immediately sizing up situations and sights, as well as determining the specific angle that provides the most effective overview. The left side of the mind knows how and why a story must be told in order to be most clearly revealed. Because the left brain is goal-oriented, the message you want to get across arrives.

PARIS LA VILLETTE.
© DENIS CHARMION.

THE PHOTOGRAPHIC IMPULSE

WHEN YOU SEE A PARTICULAR PICTURE before your eyes, the message that your left brain wants to convey might simply be the beauty of the subject. But additional details may unexpectedly appear, and the picture all but shouts another message to you. In such situations, you inevitably find yourself attempting to masterfully capture this message on film. This is exactly what happened when Angelo Lomeo photographed a road in France (below).

When I first saw the roller-coaster road, I knew I had to stop to take the photograph. But when the weather suddenly changed, as it does in France, the picture had the plus of the storm light. The photograph then became the distillation of the French countryside.

℘

LOMEO IS OFTEN DIRECTED by his right brain, which is responsible for intuition; imaginative impulsiveness; and timeless, holistic, and divergent abstractions. The picture that captures thousands of years can manifest itself at any moment, although it may require hours of waiting in one place. The resulting image often has a timeless quality since its goal wasn't concerned with definition. Lomeo describes the circumstances surrounding another photograph this way (right).

I started shooting this in the dark in Death Valley. I didn't know what would happen. And I waited. It was like theater. Then there is the balance of the lights, and the right and left of the line happened. And I knew that was the moment. And it changed in seconds. No other picture before or after would have worked for me.

FRENCH ROAD. © ANGELO LOMEO.

FIRST LIGHT, DEATH VALLEY. © ANGELO LOMEO.

ALL INDIVIDUALS ARE more or less intuitive. This trait is culturally encouraged, usually more in females than in males. So for these individuals, the right brain's ability to influence spontaneous creativity is more accessible than the left brain's analytical or rational approach to shooting. JoAnn Frank explains how she followed her compulsion to work instinctively with a random process and achieve unexplainable results in her images, which she refers to as "photograms."

For me, a photogram is as basic as placing things on photographic paper and exposing it to enlarger light or even a pen light. There is no negative. This process is unpredictable, and with a pen light even more so since you are moving and can hold the pen light at any *angle while your hand is moving. There are so many inexplicable results since you never know how light is going to pass through the objects. Light bends around the eggs. I didn't know it would. I chose the objects in the photograms solely because they are transparent, translucent, and opaque.*

I didn't know how this work was going to work out and/or what I would end up with, or if I was in the process of wasting five years. I just knew that I had to do it. If I had to think about the technical side of what I was doing, it made me feel extremely anxious. Each photogram is unique. There are no negatives. Even when I worked with the technical aspects of the work, it was secondary. I could not ever tell you what I did.

PUZZLE, 1975.
© JOANN FRANK.

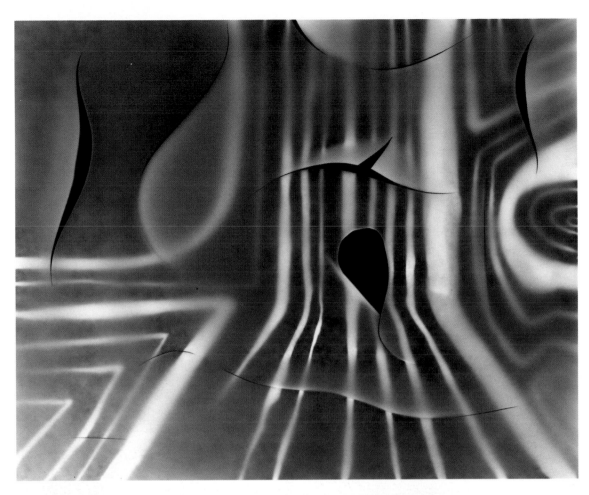

CUTS AND LINES, 1977.
© JOANN FRANK.

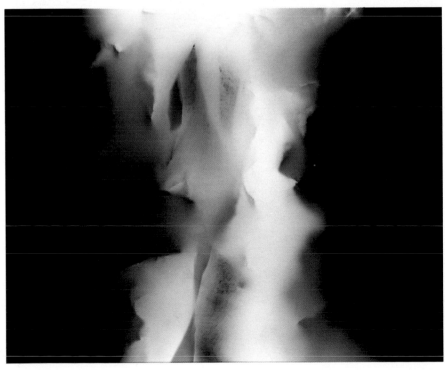

UNTITLED, 1978.
© JOANN FRANK.

RIGHT-BRAIN-ORIENTED PHOTOGRAPHS are a result of the photographers' willingness to suspend the dictates of so-called reality and suspend themselves within the moment. They don't hesitate or question when the moment to press the shutter-release button suddenly arrives. Claude Alexandre, for example, was immersed in the experience of a toreador, feeling his emotions rather than thinking her own thoughts as an observer. In other words, her thinking mind didn't get in the way of her involvement with her subject (below). Alexandre discusses the likeness of this moment to that of moments when people are able to clear their minds during meditation.

This photograph was taken at the moment of the toreador's height of triumph. He is holding both ears of the bull, which is quite rare. When I go to the bullfights, it is a very strong experience for me. A bullfighter must be alert every second, totally absorbed in what he is doing or he could die. I am totally absorbed in his every second. And after he passed around the ring with his coterie, which is the tradition, the toreador suddenly sprung up directly over the place where he had killed the bull. You can see the traces of the bull's blood and the lighter area behind him where they had pulled the bull away from the ring.

This is his passion. In its intensity, you forget yourself, your thoughts as well. This is true of any deeply passionate moment in life. That I took that photograph at that moment was "from above." I know no other way to describe it. I was there and what I saw corresponded exactly to what I was feeling.

There is a moment when I have to press the shutter release. The definition of photography is this, choice or impulse to take a photograph at that moment and not another. This choice is what gives a photograph its value. Otherwise, it is just a scrap of paper. It is that fraction of a second and taking it. And I was there.

ᔕ

IRONICALLY, ALTHOUGH YOUR EYES may be wide open, this kind of certainty about when to shoot is called "blind faith." In fact, the resulting image might be unrecognizable or only abstractly related to the actual subject. What makes an individual photographer's perspective unique is his or her vision of the world. If 100 photographers were in front of the same subject, they would shoot 100 different pictures of it. Most photographers would feel satisfied with their own interpretation—despite looking at colleagues' results and wondering whether all of them were really shooting at the same place at the same time. Some of the photographers may feel that the subject should be recognizable in the final image. But other artists may feel that the subject was merely there to evoke something in the individual artists. Jean Jacques Heuzé explains this approach, which is the guiding principle behind his work (opposite).

My photographs are of objects and have nothing to do with the function of those objects. The photographs have nothing to do with the reality but of an imaginary vision. You can see within them some resemblance to the body. When I shoot closeups of the subject

© CLAUDE
ALEXANDRE.

with my closeup lens, I discover images which are empty and yet at the same time full of material. My choice of working close up is not an aesthetic choice. There is a relationship between the object and me at the moment I look for something from it as if I were looking into a mirror.

⁓

REGARDLESS OF HOW SPONTANEOUSLY you photograph a subject, you still need your left brain. No matter how deeply the final image may emerge spontaneously from your right brain, your brain must work as an integrated whole or you may experience some rather serious problems. Without your left brain, you wouldn't even be able to pick up and operate your camera. Your approach to a subject might feel objectively analytical. However, the moment you choose to press the shutter-release button is a split-second decision dictated by your intuition. Although your choice of this particular moment may also involve such technical details as the best light, contrast, or clarity, even this judgment call is a combination of impulsive deduction.

Some photographers have found a way to cultivate the potential of both their left and right hemispheres. And there is no reason, other than preference, that anyone else can't do the same. Don't be discouraged if your efforts to be more in tune with your left-brain and right-brain tendencies are initially unmanageable and perhaps ineffective. These impulses eventually will become more familiar to you.

The exercises in this book will help you take advantage of your photographic tendencies and habits. The result: more creative, conscious approaches and, ultimately, more potential choices and more successful, satisfying photographs. You must be open to and willing to explore the various strategies described here. As you read and experiment, let your mind guide your shutter-release finger. For example, only your right brain will grasp and be able to realize the ideas presented in the section on right-brain photography. Your logical left brain would laugh at the notion of photographing music, smell, or color, while the exercises in the left-brain-photography section demand technical precision, as well as the close scrutiny of a subject before you even start thinking about how to shoot it or why. Finally, the series of exercises that integrate the functions of the left and right hemispheres requires a mixture of abstraction and precision, the literal and its metaphor.

In essence, *Right Brain/Left Brain Photography* is a book about human potential because on average, people use only 3 percent of their brain power. Furthermore, those individuals who develop one area of mental proficiency find that all aspects of their mental performance subsequently improves. I hope that this book helps to take you far enough so that you can see how to continue to challenge yourself when you shoot. However, if it takes you just a smidgen farther along than where you were yesterday, I'll be pleased. My left brain labels this progress.

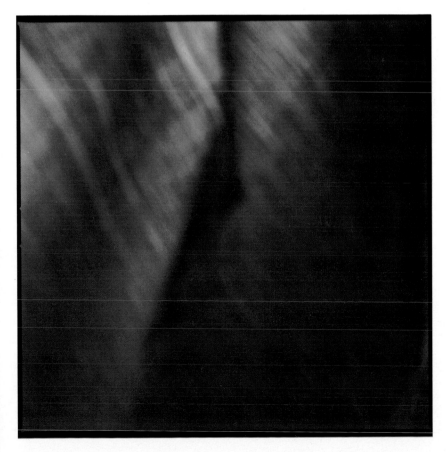

PART 1

RIGHT BRAIN
PHOTOGRAPHY

FOLLOWING YOUR INSTINCTS

THIS SECTION IS DEVOTED to suspending dictated logic, letting yourself sink into your senses, and letting your senses sink into new nonverbal ideas. There is no prescription for making a picture of a mood, a passion, or a sound. In order to express any of these abstractions, you need only follow your right-brain impulses, have your camera follow your eye, and apply pressure on the shutter-release button at the all-important but unexplainable, unpredictable moment. By doing so, you'll enable yourself to shoot what you perceive as if it were the ideal way or the only way to do it.

If you ever become blocked, all you have to do is look within. By exploring your deepest feelings, sensitivities, and fears, you'll inevitably show viewers the world as only you see it. In this way, you can't help but depict a new world. These subjective impulses are gifts from your right brain. As Ruth Bernhard reveals, it is possible to work from this deeply personal point of view often enough so that you develop a tremendous amount of confidence and have to shoot the subject on only one occasion (below).

It is the object which tells me what to do. I photograph by instinct. It is the object that is photographed which tells me that it is today that it will be photographed and like this or like that. I know how it is supposed to look before I even take the photograph. So all I do is match the vision which I already have. And I only make one exposure. There is never a second time.

This way of working works out so well. And I am simply obedient to the voice of the object. It is actually that the photograph does itself with my help. It does not surprise me at all how it looks when it is finished. It just works for me, and I feel lucky that it does. I have no doubts about this way of working. I don't make my photographs to sell; this does not concern me. In fact, I don't think at all when I'm working. My brain is not involved.

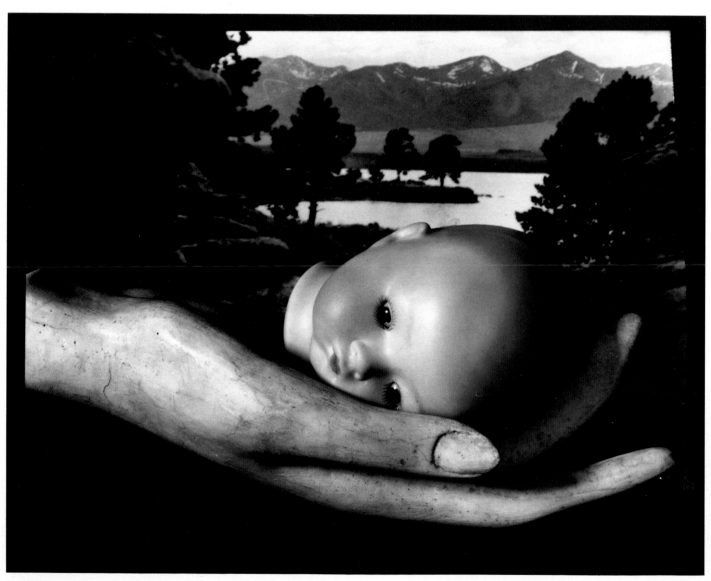

CREATION, 1936. © RUTH BERNHARD.

OUR IMPULSES ARE our most available and yet least revealed facets. They are often held within our private domain, away from public scrutiny and judgment. Brett Weston, for example, photographed primarily from his timeless subjectivity, and he worked to his own satisfaction for all of his pictures (right). Fortunately, Weston worked in response to his intuition so that he could share his instinctive sense of imagery with the rest of the world.

I see very rapidly, and I work very fast. I always photographed images for myself.

಄

DAYDREAMING, another usually private activity, offers an endless source of one-of-a-kind pictures. These photographs are imaginative, metaphorical, and definitively subjective. Contrary to popular opinion, daydreaming doesn't lead you astray; it can be one of your greatest wellsprings of self-expression if you are able to create pictures of your daydreams. If you put aside prejudgments, you permit yourself to find your uniqueness.

Anywhere you look offers a choice, whether conscious or unconscious. When letting your right brain do the driving, rather than stopping to analyze your choices, simply photograph them. In this way, you'll be free from directing your eye or your interest in any kind of logical, predictable, or justifiable course. As Sonja Bullaty makes clear, she makes her best choices when she follows her intuition, which she did while shooting a leaf (below).

I walked around with this incredible jewel of a leaf. And I felt like I needed to do something with it. It was by pure instinct that I placed it where I did. The leaf also had a feel to it. And I had such a feeling of togetherness with it. When I placed it in the cloudy water, it felt absolutely right.

MONO LAKE. © BRETT WESTON.

TWO FALL LEAVES. © SONJA BULLATY.

WHEN YOU CHOOSE PHOTOGRAPHY, a visual rather than literal art form, as a means of expressing yourself or how you see the world, you may tell yourself that you simply have a "feeling for it," a "knack," or an inexplicable satisfaction when you press the shutter-release button in order to capture a moment. You remain free from time, speech, and space while freezing fragments of time for reasons that you may or may not bother to explain to yourself or to anyone else. Irina Ionesco describes how her right brain guided the creation of a photograph of a mausoleum (below).

> You cannot go back to the same place twice. This is all the more apparent when you see a picture which is desired immediately. At that precise moment, there is a certain poetry, a presence. You know you have found the absolute landscape. What captured my eye first in this shot was, in fact, the whole picture, the perspective, the vision. I was transfixed by the little person as if caught in this mausoleum with all of its arcades. But the perspective was the integration of all of the objects in the viewfinder. It was beyond my eye. Fortunately, I had the lens that I needed that would catch my perspective, keeping the man looking so small, keeping the magic of what I saw.
>
> I have a vision as if for the theater, for I have a sense of the dramatic. This is my singularity. When I go somewhere, I transcend the moment I am living in. I go into an intermediary space, the magic side. We are not responsible in that state of mind. I am the go-between, the medium between the object (what I see) and my camera or the resulting photograph. It is the power of dreaming.

CITÉ DES MORTS.
© IRINA IONESCO.

THERE IS, IN FACT, a great deal of power in dreaming for it is in dreams that new worlds are sometimes discovered. And these previously unexplored worlds are simply unusual ways of seeing what is most common. But perhaps you feel somewhere inside that you're interested not only in familiar subjects, but also your approach to the shooting. You may then decide that rather than find words to justify your motives, you'll let your angle of shooting do your talking for you. Some of your viewers may understand, while others may not be at all convinced. So as far as viewers are concerned, either they get it or they don't. At this point, it is beyond your control, and viewers must decide whether or not to enter into this world.

Regardless, you're satisfied with the resulting imagery. In fact, you wouldn't have it any other way. Your response to your subjects was immediate. And sometimes, photographers aren't even fully aware of what they've seen and photographed until they look at the final pictures. While making a self-portrait, Eva Rubinstein experienced this phenomenon (right).

You see and take in what you don't consciously see. I photograph more than I understand at the moment. I may be seeing in a peripheral, subconscious way, but something in me sees all of the elements. It doesn't reach my conscious brain until I see the image on the contact sheet.

A student found this photograph on an old contact sheet and made the first print of it nine years after it was taken. She made me look at it, and then I understood what it was that I had not wanted to see all those years. There are always elements which we cannot see in our own photographs. If this had been one of my students' photographs, I would have seen the image differently. We just don't see as many details in our own work.

I didn't think out the taking of this photograph. What I saw was not what happened. I simply felt more comfortable in the shadows behind the chair. In the chair, I would have felt exposed, unnatural. This was really a photograph which automatically became a self-portrait. It was 1972, and looking at it now I see that it is so telling. With my arms held out straight, I am holding the empty chair before me. It is empty and I am in the shadows, but at the time I was not aware of the dust that would mystery me out in this abandoned house. The choice of the pose was impulsive, one choice among many.

SELF-PORTRAIT, RHODE ISLAND, 1972. © EVA RUBINSTEIN.

SUSPENDING THE THOUGHT PROCESS

SINCE THOUGHT DETERMINES how you perceive an experience, when you shoot from your right brain it is a good idea to simply stop thinking and become absorbed in your more impulsive side. This may sound irrational; living or working from the gut is often considered less functional and less socially acceptable. Don't let this bother you. Many abstract pictures are harder to explain than logical, concrete shots, but they can be just as compelling.

Suspending the thought process often leads to the creation of abstract pictures. However, a great deal of this photography, much like unexplainable behavior, is often more difficult to accept or justify than straightforward imagery. Nevertheless, if you let yourself react to what is around you without any prejudgment as well as without any prescribed notions about how you should

react or how the photographs should be, the present moment is yours. The resulting images will reflect this clarity. The camera provides the most direct and immediate expression of what catches your eye within a split second. Daido Moriyama uses his camera instantaneously, snatching pieces of the most everyday aspects of every day; his images reflect the world as only his eye sees it at the present moment (below).

My work concerns primarily my experience of urban life, which is translated in a direct manner which is automatic and fragmented. My photographs are extremely contrasted, out of focus, grainy, and definitively separated from realism. For me, photography is more of a means of personal expression than a tool of communication. It is a reality within itself.

© DAIDO MORIYAMA.

SUSPENDING THE CONSCIOUS THOUGHT PROCESS is quite effective. Many people do this at various points during the day without even being aware that they're doing so. More to the point, photography offers you a way to master this process and to use it to its best advantage. Denis Charmion explains how this approach affects his final photographs (below).

I look, I work with my camera, but I do not think. My eyes say "yes" when there is a symmetry of full and empty space. There is a spontaneous correspondence to this vision when the fullness and emptiness are balanced in form and color. The dynamics of form and color make the composition work or not work. It isn't worth calculating since it is strong enough where it lands in my eye.

PARIS BEAUBORG. © DENIS CHARMION.

SUSPENDING THE THOUGHT PROCESS while you shoot may seem a bit daring. But approaching your photography in this manner can enable you to produce striking and sometimes abstract images. Lilo Raymond's impulse to photograph a sheet on a window provided just such a perfect example of a powerful image (below).

> I saw light, and it was very strong. I didn't have a curtain, so I hung up a sheet. There's no object, just the light and the window. I work totally by instinct. The right angle is usually visually and emotionally satisfying. It is the right softness. It just sits right. It is simple and complicated at the same time: complicated by the patterns of sunlight and the sheet, and it balances the simplicity of the walls and window. But I didn't see this balance until afterward.

∾

WHEN UNEXPLAINABLE LOGIC dictates that the resulting image is "it," this is a sure sign that your right brain directed the shooting. The final picture might not be easily "readable," or readily defined or identified, but it is the picture that best expresses what you saw. In fact, the photograph probably involved a nonthinking rather than a calculated approach. For example, while shooting a bed, Raymond didn't pause to ask herself why or how (opposite).

> I shoot to please myself. I react to light spots. I saw the light while I was still in the bed, and I jumped up to get my camera. It was the first bed picture that I ever took. I am very attracted to white. (Maybe this is because I am from a tennis family, but it really doesn't matter.)
>
> It is instinct that tells me it is the right picture. There was a window above in the room. But it would have disrupted the simplicity. Every visual person has limited subject matter. We tend to go back to the same thing. There is a great difference between looking to be original and looking inside. The growing/evolving individual can go back to the same subject matter, and it is always different or something new.

STUDIO, 1990. © LILO RAYMOND.

BED, FLORIDA, 1969.
© LILO RAYMOND.

YOUR VERBAL MIND CAN BECOME feeling, visual, nonthinking. This is a goal that many people find very difficult to attain. Take comfort in the fact that you aren't alone. Relax, and keep trying to stop thinking when you shoot! This can lead you in a direction you had no intention of taking; it can also lead to the most inspiring of photographic "accidents." Colleen Kenyon explains how not seeing precisely where she placed herself before her lens affords her an entirely new kind of freedom (below).

I celebrate chance and accident in the photographic process. In the pictures I take of myself (using a self-timer on the camera), this comes across most clearly as the inability to see exactly where I am in front of the camera. It allows me to make freer images than I normally would. Most of my work questions family, pairing, splitting. We are always, even in an abstract way, dealing with our identity. It is this magical quality of photography that I love most, and it is why I consider myself a photographer and know that I am not a painter.

∽

ALTHOUGH IT IS HARD TO LET GO of logic, it isn't always the best guide. Furthermore, being open to your sensitivities can even seem to defy logic. But reducing the conscious thinking process can have surprisingly satisfying results in showing you a new kind of instinctual logic.

HANDCOLORED SILVER PRINT
FROM THE "COMPOSITION" SERIES,
12 X 9". © 1991 COLLEEN KENYON.

Photographic Accidents Can Happen

So-called photographic accidents can be fascinating. Laurence Brun had no intention of photographing inside this room when an unanticipated scene compelled her to shoot (below). Fortunately, as she mentions, she had the right film and the right lens to take advantage of this split-second opportunity.

I was in Afghanistan to do a photographic study on the lives of women in this Moslem country from 1971–1972. I was studying their conditions within their archaic traditions. This was a great opportunity for a female photographer since men couldn't go into most of the places where I could. I was supposed to document the life in the mountains where the houses have tiny windows cut into the earthen walls and one hole in the roof to let out the smoke and allow in a little light. When I walked into this room, I saw the whole story before my eyes in this one totally unexpected moment. The sight took me by complete surprise, the light filtering down with the dust, the expressions on the faces of the people. They so openly looked at me, a Western woman holding a camera, with their frank intrigue and spiritualism. Suddenly I just put the camera in front of my eye and took this picture.

"HAZARA" FAMILY AT HOME—AFGHANISTAN 1972. © LAURENCE BRUN.

SOME OF THE MOST left-brain-oriented arrangements profit from photographic accidents. Pierre Cordier explains the advantages of accidents within his chemigram process (below). The final images always surprise the photographer, as well as viewers.

A chemigram combines the physics of painting (varnish, wax, and oil) and the chemistry of photography (photosensitive emulsion, developer, and fixer) without the use of a camera and enlarger, and in full light. The word "chemigram" refers to both the technique and the resulting image.

Like this chemigram, my first works were random creations: I experimented with unknown localizing products, and the results were amazing or even disappointing but often uncontrolled. I was gradually able to master a large number of forms: cracks, clouds, parallel lines, homothetic surfaces, etc. Uncontrolled chance thus gives way to controlled chance. There always remains a certain amount of uncontrollable chance for it is difficult to totally control all of the elements that are required. And that is the way that it should be: I need chance; it surprises me, it stops me from doing things out of sheer habit, and it opens new paths to me.

❧

SOME PEOPLE BELIEVE that there is no such phenomenon as an accident, and that even the most impulsive or impromptu act is predetermined by the unconscious. However, when you find yourself shooting for no apparent reason, let yourself go. Your sense of self and your intuitive powers are often heightened as a result of photographic "accidents." You may see many unexpected relationships between your designated destination and the one you found "by chance." Jim Goldsmith's success with double exposures started when he accidentally put an already used roll of film through his camera while shooting in Italy (bottom).

The ultimate letting go is to take the same film and shoot it up again. When I take the first shots, I don't record what they are. I know they will be mixed with something else, but I don't know what. I am collecting, making a brew, a stockpot. I have a vague notion of the subject matter already shot on the roll when I put it back in the camera, but nothing specific. I do want a "pure" picture, such as the figures from Orvietto, to be well integrated with the second shots (which I tried to make at least from the same region more or less of Italy). But I force myself to let go. Since the other pictures are from Tuscany, somewhere there is a relationship. And I know they have never been seen in this relationship before. No matter how distantly or imprecisely, they will relate thematically. But there is no way I can predict, control, or even imagine how they will look precisely.

CHEMIGRAM
28/5/61.
© PIERRE
CORDIER.

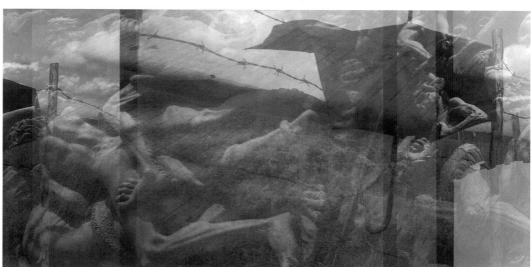

VIA ROSSA.
© JIM GOLDSMITH.

EXPLORING DIFFERENT WAYS OF SEEING

As you can guess from the countless times that you've had to rely on your instincts, they offer an endless source of alternatives. Your nonverbal intuition will never run out of different ways to see your world. During a decidedly left-brain moment, Dominique Gaessler photographed his garden from an unusual perspective (right).

I put the camera on the ground to have another vision of the garden, to have a cat's-eye view of the spectacle of nature, its architecture. I have always shot horizontally, without turning the camera, always straight ahead.

© DOMINIQUE GAESSLER.

❧

Without any verbal justification or explanation, your eye intuitively "recognizes" fragments of your world just as readily as it recognizes their more familiar whole shapes. The more you let yourself or your eye go unchecked, the more you'll feel comfortable with fragments or disassociated shapes. In addition, your sensibilities won't feel jolted by putting shapes together that are commonly disassociated.

For example, Franco Fontana sees shapes or forms within the immense design of landscapes (below). Years of shooting produces a confidence that allows the eye to follow the path of personal sensitivities. Fontana's eye is free to find a design independent of or disassociated from the overall view, no matter how intrinsic a part of the picture it may seem to be. His eye is drawn to detail and to putting the entire landscape into the one single piece.

I work on extracting geometrical forms from the natural environment. I see a slice of nature, a kind of partial abstraction of nature, a constant process of reducing the unessential information detracting from the essential elements. I have always been concerned with the dimensions of space.

© FRANCO FONTANA.

YOU MAY SEE SHAPES through the disguises of light, shadows, or angles. Shapes may also appear as a result of these factors. In these situations, disguises merely become additional shapes, as inexhaustibly varied as the directions in which you can look. If, however, you consider light changes to be a hindrance, you lessen your virtual possibilities. A "sharp" photograph has many meanings. Too often, photographers try to control the light in order to get unvarying sharpness. But as Yvonne Vaar maintains, various kinds of light offer a richness of nuances. She reveals a new dimension of the potential of light as well as meaningful applications.

My photographs deal with the vagaries of light, its willful power to expose or conceal. I am fascinated with the seen and the unseen, the overt and the hidden, the dramatic contrast of light and shadow, and how this selective illumination affects the meaning of what we see.

No matter what my subject matter, whether it be the stark, exciting modernity of a North American city, such as Toronto, or the softer, more venerable mystery of Perugia and Rome, I am always seeking these momentary revelations. They allow me to encounter impossible events in a surreal universe, peopled with dream-like phantasms and absurd juxtapositions.

"VAGARIES OF LIGHT" SERIES. PHOTOGRAPHS © YVONNE VAAR.

IN ADDITION, THE PAST, present, and future are all contained within full-feeling moments. The right brain doesn't know the restrictions or notions of time, or of a beginning, middle, or end. To the right brain, it is all one moment, one present second. Emotions transcend time as well. A photograph can, in fact, be the result of a feeling inspired by an event in your past that may reveal your current state of mind. The right side of the brain is a virtual warehouse of impulses that are scattered, not linear. As such, when you release your verbal thoughts to allow your feelings to dominate, the resulting photograph might be much greater in scope than an image produced by controlled, rational thinking.

Rather than organize a shoot according to the dictates of time, you can use time to its best advantage. You can mold time, play with it, see within it, and interpret it visually. Then suddenly you find yourself pressing the shutter-release button as you feel yourself motivated from inside. The shot could be of a subject seen as if from inside a dream, a recollection, or a projection into the future. Of course, an image that reflects the future is determined by your current state of awareness and your present point of view. As Corinne Filippi describes, awareness is a form of consciousness without words, logic, and dictates. She is in touch with her feelings rather than her objectivity when she shoots (below).

In my work, I am preceded by what I do. It is not my rationality which carries me, but my desire. When I shoot, before and during the shoot, I am not a thinking being but a feeling being. Throughout the shoot, there is a hyperpresence and a hyperabsence of the subject. There is a hyperpresence and hyperabsence since the interior "it" that shoots, does it without the knowledge of the author (I) consciousness.

Mine is a corporal commitment. I never recrop my photographs. I crop when I shoot. The setting of my pictures doesn't follow any exterior rules, but my own way of seeing. There is a moment when it is obvious that it is right, when the whole picture is there.

AS YOU EXPLORE different ways of seeing, don't be concerned that an image of a fragment might not be readily identifiable via deductive logic or found in a logical context for the mood it conveys. The photograph may still intrigue you after the roll of film is developed even though you don't remember what prompted you to push the shutter-release button. If the photograph continues to work, it is all the more to your credit since your audience surely doesn't share the same past, the same ideas of the future, or the same dreams. Furthermore, viewers are far more interested in what they find in your photographs than what you hope to share.

What you'll most likely reveal in the picture is the mood that initially fascinated you and that you hoped to record on film. Successful right-brain photography is really a matter of how deeply you let yourself experience your feelings so that you are able to convey them without your own obstacles getting in the way. If you capture the essence of the subject, there is a strong possibility that your viewers' more intuitive and instinctual side will understand and appreciate the image.

Judith Turner, a renowned architectural photographer, utilizes her intuition when she shoots. Her work goes far beyond the traditional formal approach to photographing structures; her less literal style is sensitive to the role of light, which she regards as an abstract addition (opposite). When viewers look at Turner's images, they are as likely to pick up on a mood as they are on the overall feeling of the architectural design itself.

Architecture is transformed by light. I observe that and record it. Certain materials absorb, reflect, or transmit light, and that affects our reading of forms. In traditional architectural photography, there is a preferred quality of light. I find that daylight offers contrasting formal renditions. The light at the moment of this photograph led to an ambiguous, nonliteral reading of the form. I liked that as well as the arc filling the whole frame.

ATHENES, 1989.
© CORINNE FILIPPI.

THE SENSUAL CONNECTION

ONE OF THE MOST UNIVERSAL, nonverbal, and timeless connections to a subject is your sensuality. It is also one of the greatest subtle strengths of photography. Sensuality is a sensitive, uninhibited muscle that, like a photograph, doesn't need any verbal reinforcement to be effective. As a photographer, you can be utterly connected to a subject and at the same time self-absorbed in your response to it. Often, you don't need to know the whole realistic beginning, middle, and/or end of a situation in order to adequately feel or successfully photograph the experience. These literal details can have little to do with how a clear head and clear eye can perceive or interpret a moment. And with a photograph, your viewers don't need to know anymore than you did in order for the photograph to work.

A sensual connection to your subject can, in fact, defy any logical circumstances and mutually expose you and the photographed subject in a context never before known or viewed. Remember, sensuality is based on a private, subjective, and unique point of view and is attributed to the right brain. This is because sensuality isn't fixed on an inflexible object but comes from within.

For example, onlookers are often surprised to see photographers standing in the street transfixed by a commonplace object. But the roll of telephone cable or the street lamp might be just the form that inspires their most subjective sensitivities. As Marilyn Bridges reveals, airline employees who see a particular landscape every day regard it quite differently than a photographer who is in touch with her sensual self does (below). As she points out, a sensual response comes from nonrational feeling instead of an objective analysis. As such, it is possible for a photographer to be oblivious to the specific place.

When I made this photograph, I was immersed in the energy of the moment. Working from instinct and my feeling center, I forgot that I was in an airplane looking for a landscape to photograph. Rather, I became suspended in space and communicated only with the way the sunlight caressed the earth and the subjects thereon. The instant that the light created the shapes and drama—that was the moment the earth came alive and became its most sensual. I became the huntress seeking the unknown.

JOURNEY, MONUMENT VALLEY, ARIZONA/UTAH. © 1983 MARILYN BRIDGES.

SINCE PEOPLE CAN SEE before they can speak, a camera can, for some, express the sensual beauty of ordinary objects more effectively than any words can. One of the most subjective manifestations of sensuality is rhythm; obviously, then, discerning rhythm is a function of the right brain. Shooting the rhythmic nature of landscapes and architecture, for example, can be done as you feel it. And the gracefulness of your subject will be expressed most effectively if you interpret the rhythm as your mind's eye sees it. In essence, you must leave your mind behind.

Your camera can directly record your nonliteral side with the simple left-brain function of pushing the shutter-release button. This is the beauty of having a camera to print out how you feel a dizzying sweep. The dimensions of the scene aren't overwhelming, confusing, contradictory, or distracting when you experience a subject from the less analytical point of view. When you shoot with your right brain, each dimension of the subject is seen as a united whole. This point of view also enables you to see what a trained eye or a precision instrument might overlook.

When your sensual receptors merge, you can relinquish your internal restrictive boundaries. The intellect is out of place in this situation, and realistic objectivity is wasted. Here, you need to close your eyes, in effect, and see with your other senses. This is what I did while photographing leaves in a botanical garden (below).

Although these leaves had no scent, their colors drew me to them as if they were a cloud of rich perfume. It was a delicious blending of colors and flavors: spearmint, a rich burgundy wine—a sumptuous picnic of sorts.

છ

WHEN YOU START DOING EXERCISES to tap the resources of the right brain, you'll see that it is, in fact, possible to smell with your eyes and, therefore, with your camera. Through your images, you'll be able to show what permeated the air in a field or on a beach. This will become clearer as you get more practice shooting this way. For the moment, don't consciously think about it; just let the idea sink in. In any case, the way you see is automatically affected by what you've learned and what you believe. You can't completely and permanently separate yourself from what is in your mind without severe psychosis. So while it might not be apparent to you why you react in a particular way, take a deep breath and simply leave it behind temporarily rather than fight it. In this situation, analysis will only slow you down.

Obstacles to exploring your intuitive side come in many surprising disguises. Dictated logic has many distinct disadvantages. For one, this kind of reasoning permits you to use only 3 percent of your mind's power. Theoretically, geniuses use up to 5 percent of their brain's capacity. In the meantime, the potential of your imagination and memory is staggering. As a result, there is a broad spectrum of new applications yet untried by most individual photographers. So with your camera at your fingertips, follow your most whimsical fancies. Because these sensitivities are so subjective, whatever you do will be unique.

After speaking with numerous photographers whose pictures were created with the right side of the brain, I noticed a recurring theme. The form of the photograph—the way the shot was made—and the content—what is within it—have equal importance. In fact, the form and content seem to have merged behind the photographer's eye. When a photographer shoots a right-brain photograph, any analysis of the subject would halt the relationship between the eye, the self, and the image. Otherwise, that unexplainable something inside sees the curves, shadows, and color tones come together at the same time, constituting the content and form of the picture.

© KATHRYN MARX.

EXERCISES FOR TAPPING THE RIGHT BRAIN

LET ME MAKE THE FOLLOWING POINT crystal clear from the outset. All of the exercises in this section should be done in color and black and white. Both types of film offer a wide range of unique possibilities when it comes to cultivating right-brain impulses.

DEVELOPING NONLITERAL VISION

THE FIRST EXERCISE is an introduction to nonliteral vision. This vision defies verbal explanations, thereby leaving you dependent on your free abstract impulses, your metaphorical imagination, and your unjustifiable intuition. To begin, place a collection of your newest work before you on a large surface. Next, scatter the 20 or so photographs in various directions, except the way they're intended to be viewed. In order to avoid the tendency to prejudge a "good" angle or arrangement of your subject, move around the table or area continuously without taking your eyes from the pictures.

Now stand back from several different points of view until your imaginative, intuitive right brain guides you toward seeing one united picture. You may not be able to explain exactly why the photographs go together, but impulsively you know that they do. Take several more trips around the table to find fragments that seem drawn together in the same way. Can your subjective side see several fragments that can work together simultaneously? If your answer is yes, but you can't rationally explain why, you know you are on the right track. As Nancy Wilson Pajíc reveals in her description of the process she uses to create her images, having confidence in your intuition's ability to see various pictures emerge simultaneously can produce successful photographs (below).

I took these images off of a table full of photographs. It took several days of walking around the table before I chose these three. Then I left two images on the table, one of the clouds and the hands. Then there seemed, one day, too much difference between the two images. Intuitively, I took a second cloud picture and put it on the other side of the hands.

☙

AS SOON AS YOUR intuitive decisions are made, a simultaneous presentation of your images goes further than an intellectual arrangement. Because you don't round off the corners and make your photography slick, you relinquish control to a certain degree. You have to be open in order to be stimulated by your own intuition; you can achieve this by juxtaposing photographs without any preconceived notions as to which image is most logically presented with another. This presentation is less an assemblage than it is a nonliteral vision of continuity within the multiplicity. As Mark Feldstein illustrates through his photographs, continuity can include different kinds of images; it doesn't have to be based on logical, homogeneous juxtapositions (opposite).

Photography is, in a large part, dependent on the machine. So I built some pinhole cameras for less precision. I wanted distortion and played with pinhole and panorama cameras to get linear distortion. I also decided to work with fisheye lenses. I wanted controlled images and out-of-control images together. They are more dream-like, more like the way we think. I play more with the distortion, with the madness, and then place them with controlled pictures. The two kinds of images together are more reflective of life as we live it.

LA CRÉATION. PHOTOGRAPHS © NANCY WILSON PAJIC.

We don't think in single fragments of time and space. By making a construct that cuts across different units of time and space, something else happens. I know when I shoot that they are fragments and will go into a larger piece with other pieces. The hardest part is making the constructions. I will play with them for a month sometimes. The shooting is easy.

I don't crop. I let the shots go off at the top or at the bottom because I know each individual photograph will be used with other images. The action comes in the interactions. So I let the pictures go off at the edges.

This work is closer to the way I am thinking than my earlier work. My formal end is taken care of by the sharper, more controlled images. Two out of three of the shots, I have no idea what I will get. I deliberately move the camera, so much that people think I have some terrible disease and offer to hold it for me!.

Some of the combinations are more narrative than others, some less. Dialogues are what happens between the pictures. When I am putting the pieces together of the less narrative combinations, something happens when I group them. The sum is greater than the parts. When the assemblage works, a cohesive total, a satisfying whole happens. Then the dialogue exists. If you reversed the order of the photographs, it wouldn't work because there is a sensuality to the most focused, the binoculars. And the binoculars support the upper two images. It is like the perfection of a juggling act.

For the middle image, I used a fisheye lens over a folding camera. I, therefore, had no idea where the division in the picture would be. But the top and bottom pictures were in full control. Not knowing what I will get is a real letting go. I don't know what I have until I develop the film.

BINOCULARS. © MARK FELDSTEIN.

REDEFINING FOCUS

FIRST, FIND A SUBJECT outside where there is strong evidence of changing light. Choose an area where there are plenty of shifting shadows and colors, as well as a great choice of focal points within a wide range of depth of field. You may try shooting, for example, the ever-fluctuating nature of a body of water, a park, the view out of your window, your terrace, or your own backyard.

Suppose that you're photographing a pond. Let your camera's focus adjustment function like an internal macro lens as you choose which single changing shadow, reflection, or element will be the most critical part of the photograph. The rest of the picture will then be out of focus, thereby rendering it less important. However, you may choose to shoot the element, the logical focal point of the image, deliberately out of focus. Be sure to have plenty of film for this exercise, both black-and-white and color. Shooting with these different types of film will increase the variety of the final images. You'll be able to choose among subjects that are sharp or softly focused, shot in color and black and white. Does the black-and-white film correspond to your need for flexibility more than the color film, or vice versa?

Next, shift your focus in order to shoot the surrounding body of water. Whenever your focus goes back and forth between the whole and one of its parts or details, you're automatically freeing your eye from a literal or left-brain point of view. Which composition do you prefer? As your eye moves from soft to sharp focus and back to soft while you shoot, for example, a moving reflection on water, you'll detect a change in spatial relationships. This can only help you to distance yourself even more from shooting with an objective eye; you may even start to feel your subject's movement.

CITÉ JARDIN.
© DOMINIQUE
GAESSLER.

This is a beginning to being in touch with the subjects of your photographs in an entirely new way. Training your eye to shift from a wide-angle to a macro point of view, as well as from soft focus or sharp focus, will eventually permit you to make "lens changes" from left brain to right brain at will. Dominique Gaessler explains why he didn't feel obliged to adhere to the traditional approach to photographing flowers (opposite). He spontaneously and effectively chose to contradict the expected in order to create a mysterious look at a garden. To achieve this effect, Gaessler rendered the traditionally sharp elements out of focus, and the traditionally less significant elements in focus.

In this series of photographs of the garden, the sharp photographs were shot with the Instamatic, and the out-of-focus shots were taken with the Hasselblad. This was yet another part of the illusion I was creating. With the use of the "out-of-focus" advantage of photography, I found that I was changing the point of interest, and many of my choices were unexpected. The stems are all sharp while the flowers are soft! This is a paradox, going against the classic established approach to landscape photography.

On the other hand, it seemed afterward that my approach was logical. After all, in a garden, I was revealing my ideas of what makes up the garden. I also did not want to do the same old thing. A garden is not made that way.

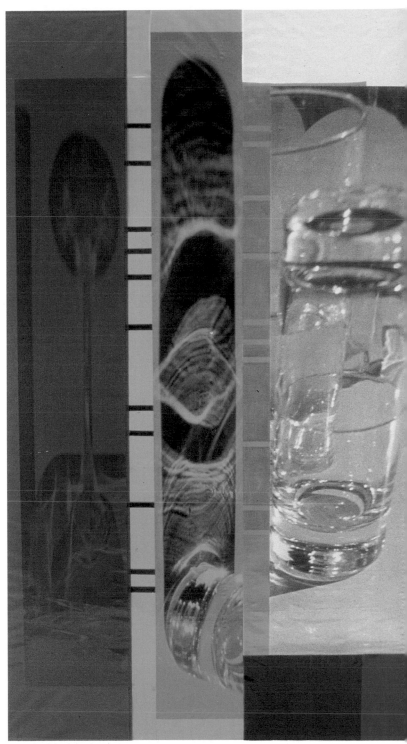

∽

DON'T EXPECT VIEWERS to be willing and ready to accept such a different look at the world. As Beatrice Delrieu makes clear, the public has had some difficulty accepting this aspect of her work (right). Because of social demands, most people respond logically rather than intuitively. But in this case, what is in focus is as important as what is out of focus.

People had trouble with my work because I had two sides, photography and painting, out of focus and sharp focus, black and white and color. I show a double reality. But it all addresses light. The shadows and soft focus are equally real. They are all opposites, but they all exist together.

This is a composition of light and color. I had a gray table, and on certain days there is a special light that gives the reflection of the glass on the table. I could see that the ambiguity of reality makes for a very fragile beauty. I shot this moment with many different glasses, a transparent material which already makes for ambiguous reality. Then it was all in relation to the false shadows and colors.

The colors are complementary. The orange, warm with yellow and red, goes to blue, a synthesis of color, cool. The shadows and soft focus exist equally with the glass. And the piece moves to the right, toward the lightness of the yellow.

IVRESSE NO. 4 (190 × 110CM). © BEATRICE DELRIEU.

PHOTOGRAPHING DREAMS

FOR THIS EXERCISE, before you go to sleep, tell yourself that you want to remember your dreams, or at least one. When you awaken, don't write down your dream in any kind of logical order of events; just make a few vague notes on the images that you recollect. The best approach would be to make a mental note of the images immediately upon waking up because most people find it difficult to recall them later in the day. After all, people are required to put their lives into some kind of logical order—often before they even get out of bed.

Ideally, you should do this exercise immediately upon opening your eyes since the images from a dream are freshest in your memory at that time. If this isn't possible, your notes will serve as a memory trigger. Only you create your dreams, so the resulting photographs will, therefore, be based on a purely subjective metaphorical foundation, relating more to feelings than to specific objects. Let yourself photograph the feeling anytime, day or night, after the dream.

Your results may appear quite different in black and white than in color, and you may select different subject matter for different films as well. Some people feel that a color rendition is too realistic for such an abstract project, while others feel this way about shooting in black and white. You may even find that you aren't choosing a "subject," but a kind of nonsubject that merely becomes a "subject" because you've framed it in your viewfinder or on paper.

For example, the "subject" may be merely part of a wall that you shoot or a misty window. While the mist on the window might reveal where you were walking in your dream, a color might throw you off completely because it will define what is, in fact, on the other side of the glass. But other people may feel that this is the very ingredient that fixes their dream image. Some individuals claim to dream in black and white, while others maintain that they dream in vivid color. Nevertheless, your choice of film depends on the precise dream you want to represent.

RIDE HOME. © JIM GOLDSMITH.

You may want to experiment with both soft-focus and sharp-focus pictures for this exercise because images in dreams can often be unclear. You may also decide to blend photographs in various directions. Within the abstract context of a dream, this will have its own right-brain kind of logic. Jim Goldsmith shows the exciting potential of going beyond trying to recapture the literal location of a dream or the actual people or events in the dream (below). Here, he manages to overcome this inhibiting kind of analysis or concrete reconstruction, which is a product of your left brain.

I am alone, traveling rapidly through a texture of light and possibility. The dream moves ahead so quickly that it is hard to focus on specific images. But I am always aware of my head as the object in this dream. So I want to make a picture of this and have my head moving through this picture, moving through this slot in time, this channel of light.

I am taking a bus upstate this afternoon. I know this is when I will make my picture. As I begin to feel this picture, I no longer see it.

I am on the bus. I had planned to use the reflection of my own head in the reflection in the window as the head of the dreamer. But now I find the silhouetted heads of the passengers across the aisle are more interesting. They do not turn but stare straight ahead.

The afternoon darkens. Now I am making a picture of the passing landscape beyond them. I do not care because I will shoot this roll of film again later when we pass the reservoir in the last glimmering of winter light. I know that this picture will work, that it will be a photograph of my dream, because I am dreaming this photograph now.

❧

AS GOLDSMITH RECOUNTS, revealing the images around him is more interesting than showing himself within his dream. Including his head may have been too objective or documentary-like. Showing what is within the head rather than the head itself provides the subjective point of excitement for both the dreamer and the viewers.

BREAKING THE LITERAL LANDSCAPE

THIS EXERCISE addresses photographing landscapes of all dimensions. In fact, this exercise is about breaking the literal landscape rather than documenting the established order. The goal is to defy the familiar by seeing it from a new point of view. This may mean photographing a fragment, pulling it from its logical whole, or shooting a wide-angle image from an "odd" perspective. For this exercise, you should allow yourself at least two landscapes, gardens, fields, forests—any splash of nature. However, you must choose one area you are familiar with and one that you don't know at all.

While photographing the landscape you know well, try to recall whether there is a particular perspective that you've always seen the landscape from, such as standing in a certain place or moving. Whether this turns out to be one point of view or several, put your eye and your camera in an entirely new position. For example, climb a tree or sit beneath a bush and shoot.

Although logic may tell you that landscape shooting requires a specific kind of composition, try shooting from the point of view utilized in one of the preceding exercises. For example, make a shadow appear in sharper focus than the surrounding "realities." Here, you don't want to see the forest for the trees.

And while logic might also dictate that you wait for a certain kind of light or for the sun to be in a particular position, you should consider an alternative approach. You may want to shoot with the sun in front of you instead of behind you, which is the traditional method. This shooting position may overexpose various parts of the picture, which can add to rather than detract from the desired effect. You might also try waiting until it is ordinarily too dark to use the film you've chosen. There is a great richness in portions of undefined subject matter in darkness.

The challenge of photographing a place you are familiar with is to render it unrecognizable. You can, however, accomplish this by shooting multiple facets of the area or concentrating on the changing light within the parameters of your macro lens. You may find that the place you know so well opens your eyes to new dimensions and to new ways of seeing. You can also analyze what changes occur when you work in black and white if you usually shoot landscapes with color film and vice versa.

Jean-Louis Vanesch describes how the world around him is merely a source of form, light, and matter for his images because he is a photographer (below). The right hemisphere of his brain permits him to take what his eyes see in the viewfinder into the realm of abstraction.

To make emptiness imposes nothing between the world and us, but leaves the connections to establish themselves. There is only to remain open to the maximum and bring images to life. My consciousness is involved only for taking care of the technicalities which permit the images to exist.

There is no premeditation in regard to the place. I only know that some are better than others. Solitude is also important. There is a progressive approach in my work. I warm up my eye the way a saxophonist does his instrument. And I know that all of the photographs in a series are only an approach. Therefore, few images show anything except arrangements of masses or the vibration of light. For me, the photograph is never taken for the sake of the subject, nor the form, light, or matter used uniquely for itself. The subject must resonate within me so that I feel the moment where the image exists. I don't live with my photographs around me. I look at them rarely. They exist to permit the discovery of the next. There can only be questions of form, light, and matter. All the rest escapes me.

© JL. VANESCH.

PHOTOGRAPHING MEMORIES

ONE OF THE MOST COMMON USES of photography is safeguarding souvenirs, the past, and memories. There are many ways to photograph the past, some of which can be done in the present. This doesn't mean, however, that you should quickly pull out your camera and take pictures of the people and places around you to protect your memory for your old age. It means shooting a recollection or a past sensation that for no apparent reason surfaces upon your viewing something, someone, or someplace in the present.

For example, you may find yourself on a lane between two rows of chestnut trees that remind you of the first vacation you took alone. You can choose to shoot the sunlight bursting through the leaves. On the other hand, you can decide to photograph the solitude and darkness of the massive tree trunks while filled with the feelings you had when you were first alone in a strange place.

Photographing memories can also mean placing earlier photographs in a radically different context in the present. What is so marvelous about the right brain's potential is its nonliteral freedom. For example, you may juxtapose a photograph of your sister on her bicycle at the age of six with a picture of you at age 30 in front of the Capitol. The placement may be determined solely on the mixed emotion that the proximity of the two images evokes; it isn't based on the specific events they record. This arrangement also serves to heighten the sentimental value of both pictures.

Take your camera and find a place that elicits a particular feeling you experienced as a child. Go to this location with your camera, and bring both color and black-and-white film. Stay in the place until those feelings resurge, then shoot. Don't photograph the area in its literal detail but the direction, for example, you're looking in while feeling these old emotions. Are you affected by the way the light hits this particular place, the sparseness of trees, the color of the cement, or the crowds of people? Sonja Bullaty has mastered this approach. As she explains, let the emotions pass through you as you look through your camera, and into your finger pushing the shutter-release button (below).

This photograph seemed to me to be about Kafka's feeling for Prague, and my feelings about Prague as well. The photograph is all feeling. I was totally absorbed in the cemetery and the feeling of my past. I noticed the green, the life in death, and then the woman walked in to support this fleeting moment of life. And this reflects my innermost feelings of my past.

DEATH AND LIFE (KAFKA'S PRAGUE). © SONJA BULLATY.

FINDING PHOTOGRAPHS from a specific past event can lead to all kinds of right-brain potential because these pictures can be changed in relation to your present intuition and imaginative abstractions. You may, for example, superimpose a second image of brown mountains over a photograph of your tenth birthday party. Another method is to cut out a portion of an old photograph and blow up only this telling fragment. The memory will never be the same!

This is a very freeing exercise because you release yourself from the literal or actual past, as well as supposed documentation. Ruth Mayerson Gilbert sees a transcending consistency in the story behind her photographs, which she shot while working in Italy. Although she creates emotionally strong images of a present moment before her camera lens, each image is timeless.

You can see the images; here is the frame. It is Sorrento; it is spring. The imagined tenor would be singing "Ritorno al Sorrento." Nearby the blue Bay of Naples, Vesuvio, Capri in the distance. On a narrow street in the old town, I see the porch of what may have been a church, framed by painted walls, trompe l'oeil tobacco fumes drift over the "Vietato Fumare" signs as the worn-out workers spend their aging days playing cards—as yesterday, as tomorrow. I see these images wherever I travel; the same aged workers take their next-to-final relaxation over the playing cards. Only the frames are different.

THE CARD PLAYERS. PHOTOGRAPHS © RUTH M. GILBERT.

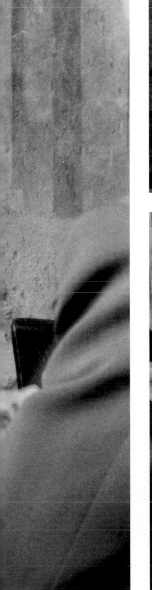

PHOTOGRAPHING EMOTIONS

ALTHOUGH YOU MIGHT NOT BE aware of it, many of your photographs are pictures of your emotions. For this exercise, don't analyze or define your emotions; you should simply visualize them. This is particularly important if you're feeling a peak of any emotion. Grab your camera and shoot. Be sure to have at least one roll of black-and-white film and one roll of color film with you.

Feelings are in a special realm. They can be affected by your thoughts but not necessarily defined or clearly described. So for a photographer, such as Lucia Radochonska, whose work is defined by the luxury—and difficulty—of working in this nonverbal mode, putting emotions on paper can be a purely abstract and impulsive means of self-expression (below).

This photograph is the first of the series which I did of a hand in water. It was only after the series that, little by little, I discovered the explanations for the work that I did. At the time, I didn't have to make any great efforts to find my model, and the water was rainwater collected in a large dark can in the garden. The model for the hand was my father-in-law, who lived next door. However, my father-in-law's hand trembled from old age, and he had to exercise a great deal of self-control to take control of the trembling. This contributed to the serious nature of the photograph, which was built into the picture as soon as it was taken. Afterward, when I looked at the images, I was greatly surprised to find how they corresponded to my ideas of a world which is worrisome and unknown.

WHEN YOU FIND YOURSELF to be in a particularly good or bad mood, that is the time to work. After you've shot the film, have a laboratory develop the rolls, but don't look at them immediately. Then the next time you're feeling an emotional peak of any kind, photograph the same subject, whether it is a person, a group of people, a place, or even yourself. Once again, have the film developed but don't look at it right away. If you mix the two sets of work, it is likely that you'll notice a difference in your approaches to the subject.

You'll see varying degrees of abstraction in the photographs in which right-brain impulses are predominant. How subjective the photographer's point of view is makes the difference. Although one photograph may be more divergent or more or less abstract than another, it is really up to the heart and eye of the photographer to determine whether to frame an intellectually conceptualized image of his or her feelings or the feelings themselves. You can feel the difference. The greater the range of emotions that you permit yourself to feel and show, the greater is your receptivity to what you see before your viewfinder. Shoot your emotions in your own way, and take your work to new visual depths.

When I made this photograph of Paris, I wasn't looking for a picture of my feelings; I wanted to be with my camera and release some of my loneliness (opposite). Taking a picture of my emotions would have been much easier because finding a picture of feelings renders them once removed. I inadvertently took a photograph that seems to evoke a sense of sadness or loneliness.

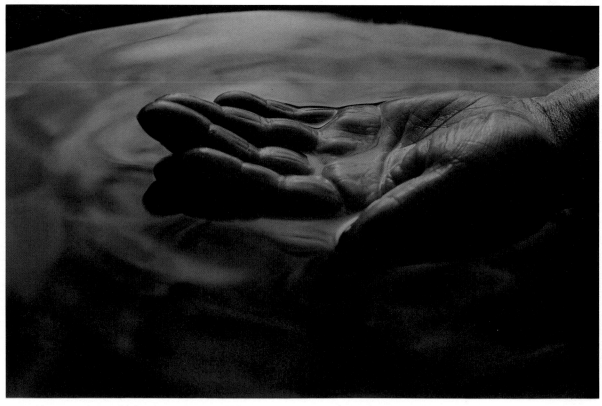

"LA MAIN DANS L'EAU" SERIES. © LUCIA RADOCHONSKA.

Nine years ago, I was living on Ile St. Louis in Paris when I was first getting to know the city, the people, and myself in this new environment. Paris rarely sees snow, so it lacks all the modern and immediate technology to remove it. Not only was I on an island in the middle of this busy city, but there was the snow to muffle much of the sound of life and keep most of the population indoors. In a peak of isolation, I took my camera to see where I was in this new world.

ↄ

Jun Shiraoka doesn't calculate the mood that emanates from his photographs (right). Like my photograph of Paris, his work is an outpouring of his emotions as he leaves himself free from concern over content. Shiraoka's strong connection to his emotions enables him to equate his senses and his intellect in his imagery. The recollection of the feelings and moods conveyed in his pictures linger much longer than that of the details.

This photograph is an image which I saw and felt. I have almost always wanted to use photography as a diary to record my experiences. Maybe I shoot when I see myself in an image and the image in myself. To take a photograph for me is to objectify myself in the photograph. I take photographs to fill an emptiness in my life. I will never fill the emptiness. I will just go on taking pictures.

I don't care about the composition of a picture. I just take a picture of a subject as I see it in front of me. I don't intend to explain a subject by its photograph, nor do I intend to give information about a subject by its photograph. Before I take a photograph, I never think what, how, or why I am going to take a picture. What does not exist for the senses, does not exist in the intellect.

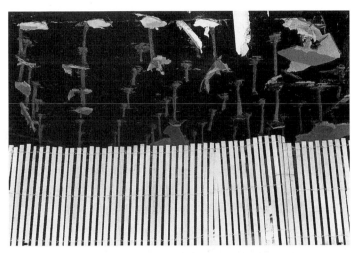

RUE DE COMMERCE, PARIS, FRANCE, JULY 15, 1987. © 1987 JUN SHIRAOKA.

ILE ST. LOUIS. © KATHRYN MARX.

PHOTOGRAPHING MUSIC

ASKING A PHOTOGRAPHER to photograph another nonverbal form of expression, such as music, for this exercise might seem like I'm pushing my point. But, in fact, I am. There is no reason that a nonverbal stimulus can't run through you and into the finger that pushes the shutter-release button any less than a visual stimulus can. If music puts you into any kind of special state or affects you at all, it is worth exploring its potential impact on your own method of self-expression.

Music has so many facets that there is a great deal of room for many divergent abstractions in this exercise. You might try photographing rhythm by capturing an aspect of movement taking place around you in colors or in tones of black and white, or by capturing something that has an abstract visual movement of its own. Whatever you come up with should enhance the music in your mind's eye.

For example, while I was shooting in a church, the choir music became a red chair (below). Although the music was particularly passionate, I didn't think of it as a red chair; I just shot what I felt. There was no literal connection whatsoever.

Churches are often filled with very stirring music. I photographed this red chair while sitting in a church in France during a choir rehearsal. The music seemed to be making mythical paths through the church's darkness. But it was only afterward, when the picture had been developed, that I noticed how the top edge of the chair seemed to be moving upward into that endless and freeing darkness.

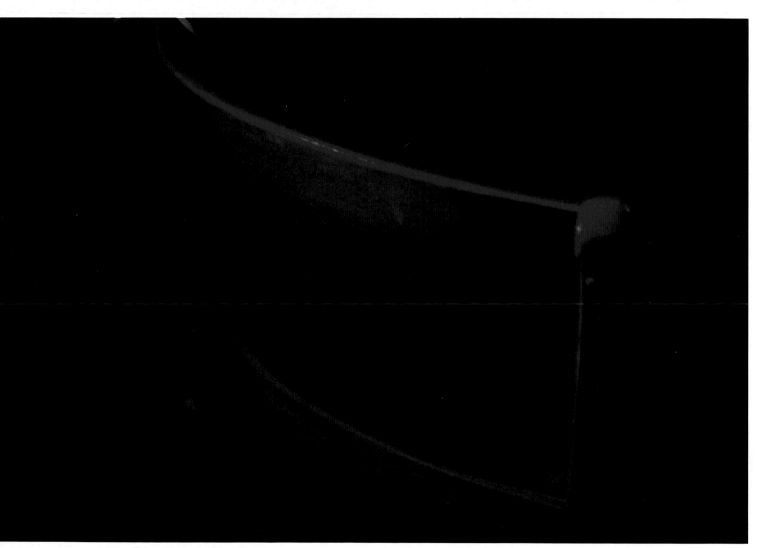

© KATHRYN MARX.

54

In my photograph, the chair merely serves as the embodiment of the feelings stirred up in me. But in Michèle Henry-Baudot's photograph of music, the expression of music is quite different (below). She saw a rhythm in the assembly of the objects, and that is what she shot.

> *Reality, for me, is actually quite small and limited. Abstraction offers the liberty of a nonoriented space, free from the thinker. Rhythm is the support of an abstract composition. It is by repetition or cadence that rhythm is created. The red batons caught my eye because of their juxtaposition, creating such a strong rhythm.*

ↄ⌀

Pierre Cordier photographed music by varying his chemigram method (right). For this variation of a chemigram, which he refers to as a "musigram," he made an abstract shot of a piece of music. This approach is uniquely Cordier.

> *This chemigram looks like a piece of music. I took the essence of a piece of music and transformed it into the musigram with the rhythm of music, the graphics of music, and the spirit of music. Music is an abstraction because without man, it would not exist. For my musigrams, it is not the code or the literal music which is important. The visual image is greater than its significance.*

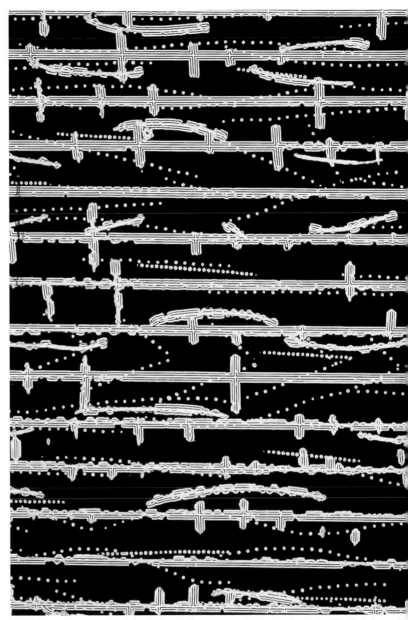

MUSIGRAM 7/3/82I. © PIERRE CORDIER.

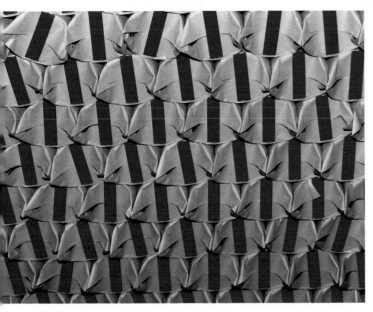

BATONS ROUGES. © MICHELE HENRY-BAUDOT.

TRANSFORMING THE LITERAL INTO THE ABSTRACT

THIS EXERCISE INVOLVES changing the familiar into the unrecognizable. As such, there are no points of reference. Your instincts are your guides, and your impulses are the tools of your imagination. Begin with a photograph or by taking a photograph of a person or a place that is as literal a reproduction of your subject as possible. Then pull apart, add to, or alter this image according to your whims. For example, you may want to work with only a fragment of the original image by enlarging only a section of the negative. Perhaps adding tints to a black-and-white image best suits the subject. Your feelings about the subject are yours to express in any way, whether this means painting horns on top of the subject's head or burning out the mouth instead of painting on a smile.

However you decide to transform the image, always make your choices with your eyes on the picture, without any justification coming from any source. Simply react to what you see, and let your impulses guide you. For example, the abstract potential of the body, which is the most literal definition of a person, provides imaginative photographers with an endless spectrum of possibilities when they exercise their intuition. Aram Dervent creates abstract images by intuitively altering his original photographs of himself; his only goal was to see where this approach would lead (below). The result can pose more questions than answers regarding individuals and their view of themselves.

This photographic collage is part of an evolution of a personal research of my identity in relationship to myself. First I photographed my body in a very classical way, being as objective and straightforward as possible. With that photograph, I thought I might be able to see what I could be and what I couldn't be. So I then separated all of the elements to reconstitute a body which was more abstract, my psychological body more than my physical body. The placement of the pieces was purely instinctual.

The tearing of the pieces of the photograph was to empty myself. There would be no preconceived notions or rules. I put the entity into pieces and into my hands. I created emptiness from solidity and then was able to construct the abstraction. I fragmented something of apparent solidity, then put it into my subconscious to build the abstraction. Destroying and rebuilding keeps it pure.

When I was reconstructing the image, I did not know what would evolve with the freedom to build in the realm of the abstract. It just came to me. The pieces took their places, and the analysis came after.

© ARAM DERVENT.

PHOTOGRAPHING COLOR IN BLACK AND WHITE AND COLOR

YOU CAN PHOTOGRAPH COLOR in both black and white and in color. Remember, photography is often referred to as "writing with light." And, obviously, color photography was around long before color film was. People knew that Rita Hayworth didn't have charcoal-gray hair and that the beaches in Hawaii didn't have black water and white and gray palm trees. For Dominique Gaessler, the color is in the image itself, and its nuances of density or texture are apparent in black and white. He explains his philosophy in his description of a photograph of a garden (below).

For me, color constructs the garden within its boundaries. This space is constant except for the evolution or change of the seasons. Although I did not want to be strictly documentary (yet all photography is documentary in one way or another), I worked in black and white. I wanted to make an allegory of an herbal encyclopedia, not the encyclopedia itself.

In keeping with the simple nature of nature, I worked with an Instamatic camera and made my own paper, like that of the nineteenth century. There is an explicit reference to a plant; however, it is the opposite of documenting since the result is not in color but in black and white, and there was no choice as to the plants since the garden grows what it can and does. It is as if I have, in fact, created an illusion.

The color was in the garden, not in the photograph. The red was documented in black and white. I expressed the color in the paper as well since I was printing on the paper which I had made like that of the nineteenth century. It has a very dense texture, the depth of the color red. I didn't need color film.

© DOMINIQUE GAESSLER.

INSTEAD OF BEING MERELY A VIEWER of black-and-white photographs that are interpreted by your mind's eye, create your own black-and-white image. Find a source of a great variety of colors, such as Las Vegas or a garden. In order to choose the color to photograph, look beyond the literal color itself to learn which elements tell you about it.

Next, shoot colors with color film. Use colors in this exercise as the primary elements rather than merely as defining aspects of your subject. Frank Horvat, for example, photographed New York in an effort to better explore and understand the process (below). Keep in mind that the sources of the colors can be as subtle as the light at the time of day that you choose to shoot, or as concrete as the mottled stone that supports a bridge.

Because I have had trouble with my eye, I have had to change from using my left eye to using my right eye. Over a period of six years, I photographed in New York based on color more than composition and balance. At the moment you aim and shoot, you invent a game and rules. If they change with each picture, it is much more fascinating. The difficulty in the series on New York was not to think in terms of situations. I was forcing myself to shoot and select for reasons of color independent of the situation. This goes against the grain of most photography. This went against my own grain!

Color is difficult for me. I do not feel at ease with color or with music. They go together. I feel insecure with color, so I am interested in the challenge of working with it. Now I do not even think in black and white anymore.

NEW YORK, 1986. © FRANK HORVAT.

PHOTOGRAPHING SMELL

THIS EXERCISE TAKES your sense of smell and passes it through your eyes. (If you prefer, you can apply this approach to your sense of hearing instead.) Of course, the left side of your mind says this notion isn't quite logical. However, this is where your right brain says, "Why not?"

First, take your camera to a place where you've experienced some of the most pleasant, or if you wish, the most unpleasant, odors. There are several approaches to photographing the stimulants of our senses in addition to a literal visual interpretation (as you saw with your photographs of music). You can shoot the source of the smell so that it is obvious to you that the resulting image captures the fragrance's essence or perfume. To your eye, to you, the picture evokes the smell.

For example, you may want to simply photograph a pot of spaghetti sauce. But to literally photograph what inspires you to eat can risk being as uninspiring as seeing the pot of sauce on the stove the morning after the meal was served. Let your other senses guide your eyes. Notice whether you execute this exercise more concretely or more abstractly with black-and-white film or color film. When Sonja Bullaty was shooting the lavender fields in Provence, there was absolutely no question (below). Her explanation as to why she made this photograph without a second's hesitation is simple and succinct, yet says it all.

This photograph was the distillation of the scent of Provence, l'essence de Provence.

❧

HAVING READ ABOUT the right-brain potentials that are innately yours, you are at least conscious of what is available to you. The applications are yours to choose. Most important, however, is relaxation. This is the key that lets you take advantage of your right brain's impulsive nature, which is an exciting and vastly unexplored entity. The resulting photographs will reveal what your inner eye discovers. In addition, you'll even develop a new way to regard your own work.

The exercises in this section will help keep your right-brain "muscles" in good shape. Practice these exercises not only in the context of this book, but also with an ongoing project or the completion of one. Use them whenever you feel that you're falling into the trap of paying too much attention to other people's judgments or your own inhibiting sense of right and wrong.

LAVENDER, PROVENCE. FROM *PROVENCE* BY SONJA BULLATY AND ANGELO LOMEO (ABBEVILLE PRESS). © SONJA BULLATY.

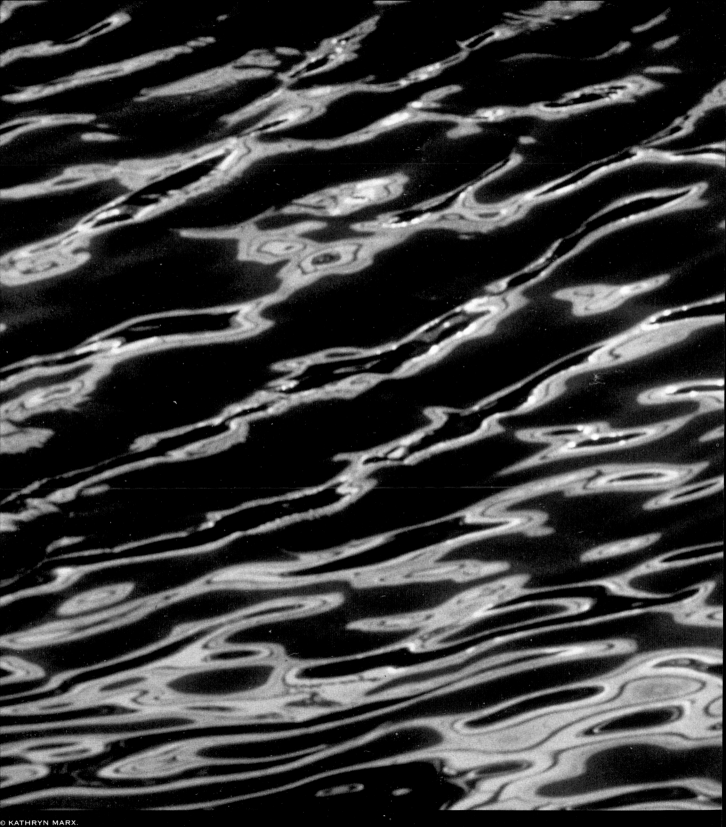

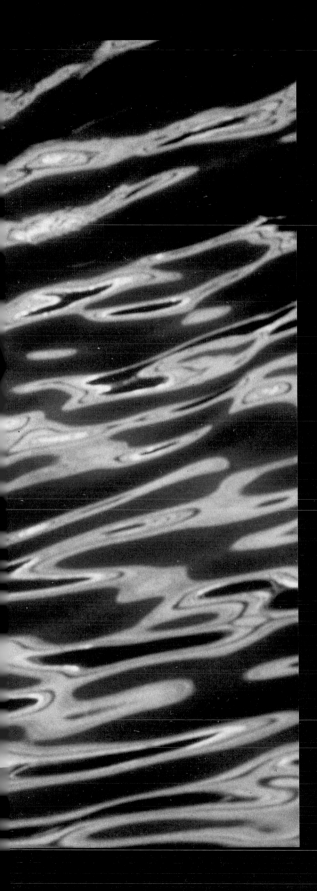

PART 2

LEFT BRAIN
PHOTOGRAPHY

ACHIEVING MAXIMUM OBJECTIVITY

LESS HAS BEEN WRITTEN about the left side of the brain than the right because people live most of their daily lives under its influence. Still, the left hemisphere is the side of the brain that most people know best and rely on. It guides their logic and their realistic, directed points of view. It is analytical, intellectual, objectively explicit, and concrete, as well as socially acceptable.

Left-brain-oriented pictures, such as medical, sports, industrial, and journalistic photographs, take nothing for granted. They're shot as faithfully to the surrounding reality as possible. The certainty here is a maximum of objectivity. Any sociologist will confirm that there is no such thing as complete objectivity. But the left-brain-oriented photographer's efforts are directed toward exposing the facts rather than the fanciful aspects of an event; the same holds true for capturing a person or place in context. All are defined with great precision. Then after the photographer shoots the image, the left brain potentially manipulates or enhances the final image. Since the left hemisphere is the verbal half of the brain, left-brain photographs can "speak" to a wide audience.

When you're asked to shoot a baseball game or a ballet, the goal is to show or tell of an important moment or series of moments so that viewers can understand exactly what happened. In other words, your job is to shoot with your left brain and follow the sequence of time. The right-brain approach, on the other hand, would be to capture the entire sequence in one interpretive glance. However, when an explicit picture is in demand, this request is fulfilled by the left brain's power.

This power can be thrilling when it is directed effectively, such as in Martha Swope's photographs of ballet dancers (below). The left brain's capacity for profound accuracy can, in fact, take you higher as a photographer rather than hold you down. Swope catches the most dramatic or the peak moment of a dancer's leap in order to meet the demands of her enormous public. The precision in her images is breathtaking.

If you have had the dance training, you have the kinesthetic sense and body response to anticipate what is coming in the leap. Even your body responds as well as the eye.

GEORGE BALANCHINE AND SUZANNE FARRELL IN "VARIATIONS," 5/66. © 1990 MARTHA SWOPE.

As MENTIONED EARLIER, people are more familiar with their left brain than their right brain. The left brain is responsible for the verbal, intellectual façade that they present to the world, while the right brain is the source of the often-disguised gut reaction, as well as their more secretive self. The left hemisphere is simply less obscure than the existential right brain. However, the imagery resulting from either approach can baffle viewers.

Don't mistake left-brain photography for the thinking person's photography. It isn't that photographers shooting from the right brain don't think. They merely think a different way or are in a different or less "logical" state of mind. The left brain manifests externally oriented deductive or rational tendencies. I say "externally oriented" here only because when you use a left-brain approach, viewers are more likely to recognize your subject, as well as why you shot it the way you did.

Furthermore, people often prefer the familiar to the unusual. Most readers, for example, prefer a well-constructed suspense story to an offbeat novel. Similarly, it is easier to find a public for a photographic series on a news event than for a series of abstract interpretations of lily pads. The audience's eye focuses on a concrete, precise detail in left-brain-directed photographs. Martin Sheerin uses the traditional black-and-white approach to document events at a Pentecostal church (below and at right).

This photograph was well thought out as to how I could best set the scene for the story. The series of photographs was taken over a period of time at a mainly Hispanic Pentecostal church in East Harlem, New York. During the summer, the church is taken to the "street." The only way of creating the "opener" photograph was to get onto the roof of a surrounding building.

CITYSCAPE 1. © MARTIN SHEERIN.

CITYSCAPE 10.
© MARTIN SHEERIN.

LEFT-BRAIN-ORIENTED PHOTOGRAPHS are based on realistic images. Because the pictures are explicit, the images appear logical and understandable. Sometimes photographers are required to put forth guidelines in order for viewers to follow their logic. But left-brain photographs communicate their meanings with few obstacles. Georges Rousse often includes written messages within his photographs (below). His work is carefully thought out. He even builds the interior sets of the buildings he shoots. Determining their environment provides him with another clean slate for his statements and reinforces what he wants to say. Although his images might appear surrealistic rather than realistic, they're deductively and discreetly framed to make his points.

My intention is to construct, to make a sculpture which one only finds beyond a mirror. In some ways, I work with the invisible.

The buildings where I work are abandoned and are either going to be torn down or totally renovated. Just before they are, I hope to give them a higher function, something sacred, a difficult word to use.

These buildings have no historical or architectural interest. I live in a city where death is all around me. These abandoned places are for me like a gap, a tower which goes up to the sky, an opening. I must climb up in order to breathe. Each time that I do this work in one of these buildings, it is an opening in the society for me toward the heavens.

I clear out the building before I work in order to empty it of its past and make it pure. I then look for my relationship with the space. It is necessary to try to find the forms, the dimensions to create a ladder between the space and myself. I am looking to discover light in these sordid places.

© GEORGES ROUSSE.

Shooting with a Purpose

Despite photographers' best efforts, even intellectually directed pictures can perplex viewers. To eliminate this problem, it is helpful to shoot with a specific purpose. Although Teun Hocks employs his imagination, his left brain's explicit deductions guide it when he shoots. His pictures illuminate the potential dominance of sequential rationalizing over his right brain's impulses (below). He explains how he "works" to convince viewers of the authenticity of his photographs. Hocks's ultimate goal, which he channels all his efforts into, is the creation of a sense of reality.

I enter the realm of artifice, a universe where a magician performs his tricks and stage-manages his act so that the performer obtains the spectator's suspension of disbelief. This is the prerequisite to the brutal awareness that reality will boomerang back in his face. I work to convince the viewer that what he sees is true before he has the realization that he has been fooled.

I invent my photographic situations. Starting from the sketches, I make drawings of the situation as I wish to photograph it. I produce them, and I am within them as the protagonist. I have control over the set while I also play the character to whom everything seems to happen in a world where natural laws seem to no longer apply, where the everyday resembles a fairy tale. Then I take the picture in black and white. After blowing it up, printing it, sepia-toning it, and sticking it on wood, I use transparent oil paints to color the photograph. With the use of color, I can enhance the atmosphere and create an extra opportunity for molding the situation to my will.

I am the actor and the stage director completely absorbed in my own play. My images represent emotional states that often illustrate the awareness of failing again and again. Because the final result remains a photograph, there is a sense of reality that intensifies the situations depicted, making them more harrowing.

UNTITLED. 122 × 155CM. © 1991 TEUN HOCKS.

THE VERTICAL PERSPECTIVE is attributed to the left side of the brain. Unlike a subject captured by the right brain's continuous and straightforward horizontal perspective, a subject photographed vertically can be quite compelling. This somewhat unusual format leaves less room for viewers' eyes to wander in the frame. And the angle at which the shot was made serves to further emphasize the focal point of the image. When a client gave Marilyn Bridges a specific assignment, her left brain enabled her to successfully realize the designated goal (right). As requested, she photographed the subject so that the building cuts a clean vertical slice in its surroundings.

I was on an assignment to shoot New York architecture when I created this photograph, and was fully aware beforehand of the object I was looking for. This formalized my approach to it. When I saw the Chrysler building below me, I decided that a vertical composition would best fill my frame, and I figured out how the light would sculpturally enhance the building's cold, geometric beauty. Thus, a totemic message could be pulled from the subject and shared effectively with others. I was fully aware of the impact this photograph would have on a greater audience than myself.

❧

WHEN YOU'RE WORKING on a photographic assignment, keep in mind that this isn't the time to suspend your sense of reality or slip completely into your imagination. The client wants every ounce of your social awareness, as well as a realistic, practical, and concrete application of your camera. The client's product, whether it is a building design or a bar of soap, should be separate from whatever you choose to show around it. Your imagination can play a role in such shooting situations, but it must be secondary to both a strong sense of purpose and a clear intellectual awareness of the client's demands. Ron Lowery understands full well the importance of having your left brain harness your right brain's impulses and keeping both tightly linked to clients' demands (opposite).

My ideas come from day-to-day activities and especially unusual and dramatic surroundings. For instance, after meeting with Richard Steedman of the Stock Market in New York one day and discussing laser- and fiber-optics technology, I ended up later at the plaza between the World Trade Center towers. As I was sitting there eating a snack, I noticed the large, round marble slab with people casually walking around. During the trip home, I mentally converted the marble slab to a laser disc and the business people to ruby lasers that were reading and writing information to the disc.

After 25 years in commercial photography, it is sometimes a struggle to turn loose of realism and old formalities. While a lot of people are trying to create photorealism with a computer, I sometimes find it a mental barricade. True, the refractive index of a diamond is 2.6, but why not try 12!

This image with the green staircases was made to represent people's various objectives or goals. I positioned these people on the staircases to represent different lifestyles and situations. The man who is crawling is a superachiever. The one who is walking up a regular staircase has a livable level of ambition. The woman is unsure of her direction and could be going in various directions.

This image is being marketed by Tony Stone Images. It has already sold over 40 times. In a three-year period, this image will probably sell about 200 times. It was four years ago that Tony Stone told me that staircases would be a hot topic for stock sales. Although I began work on one right away, it simply wasn't coming across with the power I had envisioned. The image stayed on the back burner for two years until new software and inspirations helped make it a reality. There are situations when I need time for the concept to be worked out in my head, and I will therefore work on as many as 12 images at a time.

CHRYSLER BUILDING, NY 1988. © 1988 MARILYN BRIDGES.

GREEN STAIRCASES. © RON LOWERY.

YOUR DISCRETION (or lack thereof), your objectivity, and your daily goal-oriented activities are guided predominantly by your left brain. If you want to create a photographic editorial or make a political comment or a statement about life in today's society, for example, exploit your intellectual and historical left brain. It is your best guide when you're shooting with a purpose. Mary Frey chose a left-brain approach to express her opinion about the roles women are sometimes forced to play through her photography (below left).

These photographs reflect the concerns that have always informed my work. The female body, in our visual heritage, has represented many ideas. It is seen, at times, as idealized beauty, symbolic power, commodity, and sexual object, to cite a few. Because of its rich and varied history, I have chosen the image of the female body to dissect and/or dismember visually. The large body images are meant to appear cold and clinical, reminiscent of laboratory specimens, or archive or catalog photos. The pictographs beneath are composed of photographs that are gathered from other informational sources and are intended to function as texts.

Each piece relies on the symbolic juxtaposition of the collage image for its "reading." Seen in its entirety, the series of "Body/Parts" comments on the various roles (parts) that are thrust upon women

during their lives. Issues, such as identity, commitment, narcissism, intimacy, and control, are explored or challenged. My hope is that each piece is clear enough in its content to suggest such ideas, yet ambiguous enough in its form to allow for multiple layers of interpretations.

❧

I WOULD LIKE TO UNDERSCORE once again the point that neither the left nor right hemisphere guides you alone. But one side of the brain is usually dominant. Suppose, for example, that a photographer is shooting images for a business brochure that show a product clearly and objectively. The photographer's right brain is the source of the creative inspiration, but the left brain dictates the final image, directing it toward the designated or precise purpose. Simon Fulford had a specific goal in mind while photographing some disabled individuals (below right).

My objective was to use photography as a sociological tool to document and facilitate the integration of people with developmental disabilities into our communities. Working on the premise that people with disabilities are excluded from mainstream imagery, I turned my camera toward this population so as to expose the

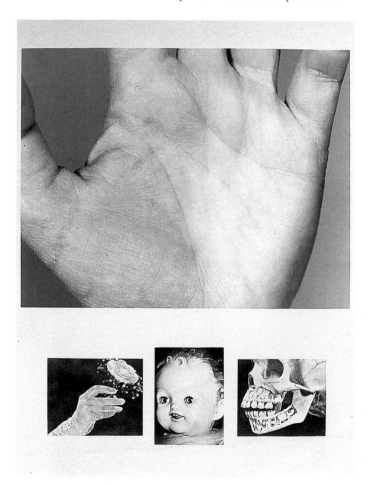

NUMBER 5 FROM "BODY/PARTS" SERIES, 1989-91. © MARY FREY.

PORTRAIT OF BRIAN MORRIS. FROM "PORTRAITS OF PEOPLE." © SIMON FULFORD.

greater public to the overlooked commonalities between people with and without disabilities. Since they are generally portrayed in pity-evoking imagery, I wanted to empower people with disabilities by changing the way that this medium depicts them.

My first approach was to show people with disabilities doing very day-to day activities, like cooking, working, shopping, and socializing. I hoped to make the viewer realize that this is not amazing or superhuman, but simply how everyone has to live—regardless of their abilities. However, I realized that this had the potential of backfiring and eliciting the usual pitying statements, like, "Oh, isn't that nice, a handicapped person cooking." The more I thought about it and the more I tried approaching each person as an individual, the more I wanted to cut out all extraneous information and concentrate on what was in front of me, a person. Nothing more, nothing less.

This is when I began simple portraiture. I focused entirely on the person in front of my camera and elicited their active involvement in choosing how they wanted to present themselves to me (and to the rest of the world). I did not focus on the wheelchair or the braces, the group home, institution, or apartment, the job that they were doing, or the activities they were involved in.

Like Ron Lowery, Jim Goldsmith was also given some guidelines by his stock-photography house, Photonica. The subject was as vast as time itself. However, with a few more precise suggestions, Goldsmith filled the bill (below).

Photonica, my stock agency, said that they needed unconventional images about time and what its effect is on people. So I composed this photograph working with videos. First, I went out and shot the piece of plywood with red paint for the background so that the rest of the images I shot would be trapped within the grain of the wood. Then I shot the clock and train on the first exposure of the film from the movie. This image was superimposed over the photograph of the wood.

On a third exposure, I shot the hands from another movie. I wanted to get the image of somebody who was worried, anxious about time, or late for an appointment. That is the context in which images about time are used the most frequently in corporate publications concerning organization of time. The hands seem to be fidgeting with worry but could also be seen as calm, waiting for the train or for time to pass. This is definitely a businessman's hands because of the suit and shirt cuff. This photograph sold immediately and has done well ever since.

TRAIN TIME. © JIM GOLDSMITH.

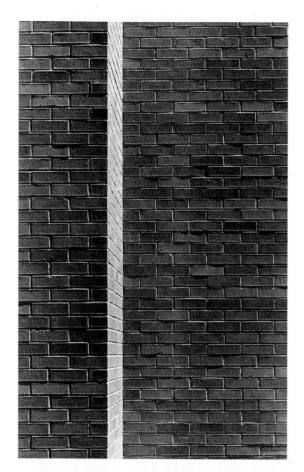

THE COVER
OF *TROPISM*.
© RALPH
GIBSON.

JOY, PARFUM. © ANDREAS MAHL.

OF COURSE, SOMETIMES your purpose is the most basic one of all. Your only goal is to create a halting piece of imagery, a photograph that makes viewers stop and look—and look again and again. Ralph Gibson describes the goal he had in mind while shooting this image and how he went about accomplishing it (left).

This photograph was made to produce optical flotation. It is a trompe l'oeil. If I moved at all to the right or the left, the photograph would not have worked. This photograph required a 90mm lens and pinpoint precision.

☙

IF YOUR JOB IS TO MAKE a product seductive to a particular audience and you know what that audience finds seductive, your left brain will offer the polished guidance of know-how. Some call this calculated manipulation. I think that is it exactly. And isn't this precisely what the client wants? As Andreas Mahl reveals, this kind of left-brain practicality can be very handy—and the resulting images quite effective (below left).

This photograph for Joy perfume was done for Passport *for Air France, which has an advertisement for Joy perfume. What counts, of course, is their product, therefore the arrangement, the presentation. I put the bottle of perfume with a very red Jean Patou scarf (made by the same manufacturer as the perfume). This scarf functioned as a dramatic opera curtain. I chose the red because it is a rich color that speaks of elegance and sophistication. The gold jewelry, handbag, and earrings speak of the same.*

The earrings and bracelets are on the left because in photographs, the viewers' eyes move toward the right. So that which is placed center right or right of center is the most important element. I had to create the lines of vision in the piece which corresponded with the geometric lines balancing all of the elements, especially around that most important point of interest, center to right. I also wanted to build the contrast between the bottle, which is square, and the round objects around it.

At times, you feel the right form or shape. This is uncalculated. But it becomes a habit. It is rare when I say, "This is perfect." I am not easily contented. I think I can redo it better. In the composition, I concentrate on the one expression. If I move around the elements too much, it never works. I put the elements together and do not go further except with color. I know the elements, how many, but I try different colors, for example different handbags or different scarves. But I know I will have those specific elements in the photograph from the very beginning. In fact, the most difficult part is not the arrangement but taking the picture, integrating the best lighting with the arrangement, for example, or choosing the right film. Then it can happen very spontaneously and work. Other times, it can be very studied and not work at all.

Two shots are never the same with Polaroid. There is a certain amount of time that the picture develops before pulling it out of the camera. That can vary. I cannot always calculate. I have to do several. The quality of color decides which is the best. Ultimately, it is the technical elements which determine which is the best.

DESIGNING EFFECTIVE IMAGES

BECAUSE THE LEFT BRAIN is responsible for human verbal potential, photographs guided by the left brain tell a story in a logical order with a beginning, a middle, and an end. When the left brain imposes this structure on an image, it can't help but be effectively designed. Kathleen Kenyon's picture succeeds because it contains these essential storytelling components (below).

Charmed from childhood by stories in books and magazines, in 1992 I created a set of images using True Story magazine pages from the 1920s–1970s, rephotographed imagery, paint, and Plexiglas—as a surrogate diary—to showcase media myths and cultural fantasies. The mythical stories from the magazines became my stories. Literally, their pages became chapters of my life. Fantasy, sleep, tears, and the bedroom-as-testing-ground became my subjects. The True Story pages are meant to be stern warnings, gentle reminders, ludicrous rejoinders—the messages women receive need to be reviewed.

GOODY TWO SHOES. PHOTOGRAPHS, PLASTIC, PAINT, 15 × 35". © 1990 KATHLEEN KENYON.

WITHIN THE VIEWFINDER are all the elements that you need to build a cohesive image. A picture can speak out loud and clear. The language of a left-brain-oriented photograph is its content, which is further reinforced by its form or the well-thought-out way the shot is made. With an impetus from the left brain, you can design the light, lines, and angles, and ultimately manipulate the image for maximum effectiveness. Ralph Gibson describes the left-brain approach he used for a dramatic photograph of a woman (below).

This photograph is the result of a fortuitous consubstantiation of diverse elements. I saw shadow and white. I carefully composed the ocean. I didn't want her nose to go above the horizon line.

I asked her to hold the pose. If we always shot this way, we would have a masterpiece each time. I knew I had isolated a band width of visual intelligence for which I yearn. I see in shapes and values. I recognize negative space. The negative shapes are produced by the object itself. Above all, I never work without thinking.

෴

BEING CONSCIOUS OF the technical feats your camera-machine makes possible in relation to your surroundings or a specific subject can change them for you as well as for viewers. (I use the term "camera-machine" here because with all of the new automation, it is very easy to forget that a camera is, in fact, a

UNTITLED. FROM THE "BLACK" SERIES. © RALPH GIBSON.

FENCES VIII, NEW YORK CITY, 1988. © 1988 JUDITH TURNER.

machine that you can operate in such a way that it suits your specific needs.) It is the left brain's job to cope with the precision of the camera-machine's mechanisms. With this kind of awareness and know-how, you're equipped to create an endless spectrum of striking images. Judith Turner shows the effectiveness of taking goal-oriented manipulation one step further. Her left brain masters the camera in order to create the desired images, and then she realizes an equally clearsighted goal in her final picture (below).

In this picture composed of multiple images, the subject matter is photographed in one order and restructured by a different arrangement. This manipulation and forced integration of the object expresses a new intention. The fence becomes my fence.

When you walk by, there is only one place where you can see through the slits between the two buildings. Here, the point is repeated four times. When I move, the slit moves, changing its form. I like the three-dimensional perspective. I also like that it is a foreground shot. The repetition gives a different sense of space.

Between the third and fourth images, it almost looks like you are turning a corner, seeing something from two angles. Yet, in fact, it is a frontal shot. This is an image repeated, but not a repeated pattern because it is repeated in a different way each time. I knew these photographs would not be used as single images but as multiples to create one larger picture. It is a restructuring, a re-presentation of the fence.

INTEGRATING CONTENT AND FORM

ALTHOUGH A PHOTOGRAPHIC IMAGE is literally a nonverbal means of communication, it can speak volumes. Photographers guided by their left brains first pay attention to the picture's content. They make sure that the meaning, whether personal and/or universal, is clear, and that all of the vital elements are included. The left side of the brain then guides the execution. As Bernard Faucon reveals, effectively reaching his audience is determined by the clarity of the intellectual approach to his photographs.

There is a great deal of calculation behind my photographs so that my viewers who will view my photographs are able to feel the passion that I felt at the beginning of the pictures' conception.

In this series, "Idols and Sacrifices," I did not imagine the couplets of photographs or their arrangement at all. I did, however, *have the series in mind from the beginning. I decided to light them (the idols and sacrifices) with strong light. There was a flame, approximately 3 yards high at night. Of course, they could not look directly at the light, but I asked that they at least look toward the fire. When they did so, they looked lost or pained. They looked like idols, and one never knows if the idols are to be sacrificed or victorious.*

They are all golden as a result of the fire. I was looking for the specific look that I wanted. I tried shooting the boys with their eyes hidden at first, but eyes communicate all of the passion. The boys could also not look directly at the lens because it would have been too much like a portrait. The only way was to give them something to look at which was impossible to look at.

LES IDOLES ET LES SACRIFICES—LE PORTE DE MYCENES. © BERNARD FAUCON.

The landscape: There is a stream running red, like blood, throughout the series. I wanted blood idealized. It was more an idea of blood than an attempt at its representation. I put cement at the bottom of a trench that I dug, then added red pigment and 600 liters or so of water to mix with the pigment. I found the area with the boulders. I then destroyed a small grove of trees which was too close by.

This work was based on several ideas. All of my work before was about representing what is alive. We only photograph what we love, and that is alive. But photography, in fact, assassinates its subject, because it saves only an instant. But photography always wants the magic repeated in the image. Yet this cannot be done. It is unphotographable. So I tried to capture the living with calculations, with my dummies, etc. I found that it is the absence of life which keeps it alive.

With the "Idols and Sacrifices" series, I went directly to the body, the living. But it is something that I knew at the beginning was to be a way to show the living with the landscape of sacrifice, the sacrifice of photography. It really is preservation by absence.

Placement of the photographs: We remember what we see on the right side. Then, after seeing the idol, we keep that in mind and then look at the landscape. The landscape sends us to the idol where we stay. The idol is more important. Landscape is just the key. The subject is the idols, and the landscape is only there because without the idols there would be no sacrifice.

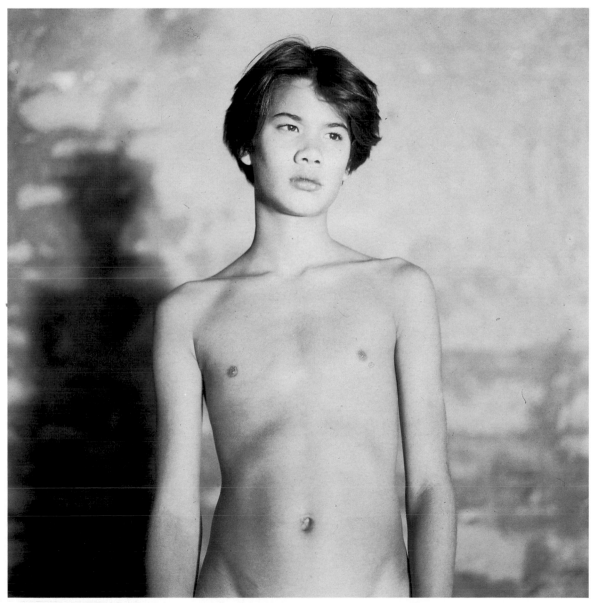

LES IDOLES ET LES SACRIFICES—ANTOINE. © BERNARD FAUCON.

THE FORM OF A PHOTOGRAPH should enhance or reinforce rather than obscure the content's effectiveness. This is logical. When you prepare a speech, you must first consider what must be said. Then you decide how to express these thoughts in the most forceful, intelligent, and ultimately coherent way possible. These abilities are all gifts from the left side of the brain that organize an image through which you communicate a specific message. The result: a smooth integration of content and form.

When Lucien Clergue shoots, he arranges the elements in his photographs so that each individual component is underscored when the image is viewed as a whole. He makes his considerations of placement and balance quite clear to produce the strongest, most integrated image possible. Clergue's success is perhaps most evident in his photographs of female nudes (below).

The nude photograph was taken in the Mountain of Sainte Victoire under a waterfall. I placed the model below so that she brings forth the wet rock at the middle of the image, and that she receives the water which fell from above. The body is cut at the top of the neck because I did not want to show her head in order not to identify her. At the left, the right thigh enters and disappears under the left in order to balance a lateral triangle, which leaves at the point of her breasts and comes to pass away between her thighs.

NU DE LA MONTAGUE
STE VICTOIRE, 1971.
© 1993, LUCIEN CLERGUE,
ARLES, FRANCE.

WHEN YOU SHOOT A PHOTOGRAPH to most effectively express or show something, you approach your subject, whether it is a place, a situation, an individual, or several people, with certain prejudgments or expectations. The left brain then provides you with a kind of internal deductive narrative. This rationalization process, complete with a beginning, middle, and end, enables you to become quite familiar with your subject before you define it through the lens. David Heald, for example, studied the abbey's architecture in order to faithfully capture it on film (below).

I seek to go beyond the purely literal image to reveal and define the subtle relationships between the audible and the visible. The builders of the abbeys often used the numerical ratios of music as a basis for calculating architectural proportions. Their simplicity of design and rigorous use of geometry form a direct link to many of the issues facing twentieth-century artists and architects. I create photographs which quietly evoke the profound unity of design and acoustics for which these buildings are known.

ABBEY OF LE THORONET, FRANCE. © 1993 DAVID HEALD.

THE LEFT BRAIN HAS the potential to place the given information in a sequence of pictures. As a result, you can reveal your subject so that it is best understood by an unknowing or unsuspecting audience. You may then decide that a series of photographs isn't the most effective means of communication; it is merely a jumping-off point for your work. The ultimate goal of the left brain is to achieve clarity—to pull information together coherently and cogently.

The left side of the brain also provides you with the means to present a precise image of your subject, whether you analyze the subject for a definitive single picture or shoot a well-thought-out succession of shots in order to reveal the analysis itself. Your left brain is your logical fine-tuner, which offers you a realistic approach to photography. Furthermore, this method is at your disposal whenever your left brain dictates that a straightforward

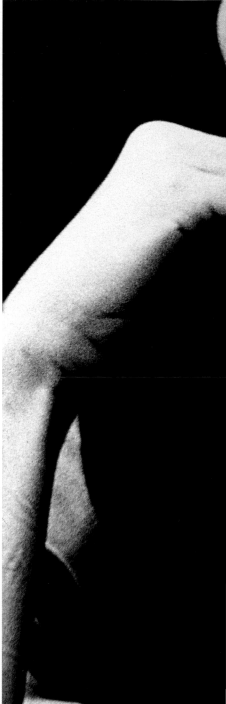

image is best suited to your subject. This strategy worked quite well for Nancy Wilson Pajíc, who carefully arranged a study of a relative's hands.

This idea of working on the gestures of my grandmother's hands and my own was set up in advance. I posed the pictures and then arranged the sequence for a good overall composition. I chose a small format because the photographs are documentary.

YOU CAN BE SURE THAT your left side of the brain will speak up when your work calls for clearsightedness. The left hemisphere's goal is to communicate. And as soon as you tap this tool, your images will reveal a new, solid decisiveness; clarity will be within your grasp. The strength of what you want to say through your photography is simply a question of exercising the innate gifts your left brain has to offer.

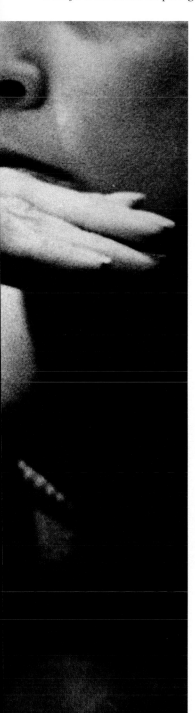

WHEN I WAS YOUNG, MY MOTHER FREQUENTLY REPRIMANDED ME FOR TOUCHING MY FACE. MY HANDS, WHICH WERE USUALLY DIRTY, WERE CONSTANTLY IN THE VICINITY OF MY MOUTH AND I WAS RUINING MY COMPLEXION.

RECENTLY I REALIZED THAT THESE GESTURES WERE LIKE MY GRANDMOTHER'S. SHE HAD SURVIVED A DELICATE NERVE OPERATION WHICH HAD NUMBED ONE SIDE OF HER FACE, AND SHE WAS AFRAID THAT FOOD OR SALIVA MIGHT ESCAPE FROM THE CORNER OF HER MOUTH WHERE SHE COULDN'T FEEL IT.

FROM MY GRANDMOTHER I LEARNED TO HIDE MY REAL FEELINGS FROM PEOPLE WHO WOULD HAVE LIKED TO BREAK MY SPIRIT. OFTEN IT WAS ENOUGH MERELY TO MASK THE EXPRESSION ON MY FACE.

EVEN LATER I LEARNED THAT THE TRIFACIAL NEURALGIA WHICH HAD NECESSITATED MY GRANDMOTHER'S OPERATION IS PROBABLY CAUSED BY UNEXPRESSED NEGATIVE EMOTIONS.

COVERING MY FACE:
MY GRANDMOTHER'S GESTURES.

COVERING MY FACE (MY GRANDMOTHER'S GESTURES) 1973–4 (DETAIL). PHOTOGRAPHS © NANCY WILSON PAJIC.

EXERCISES FOR TAPPING THE LEFT BRAIN

DEVISING A LITERAL INTERPRETATION

ONCE AGAIN, YOU SHOULD do all of the exercises in this section in both color and black and white. The purpose of the first exercise is to define a subject, whether a person, place, or object, as literally as possible with photographs. You can record a sequence of events during, for example, a basketball game, a political rally, or an afternoon in a park. Make sure that your depth of field and focus are well-directed to capture what you think are the most important details. Be as precise or as explicit as possible. Then with the developed pictures, describe what you've seen very specifically. Andreas Feininger was confronted with this challenge when shooting a new type of helicopter for *Life* magazine (below).

This photograph was completely controlled. I even told the pilot which way to fly. I was not sure what shot I would get, but I followed the progress of his flight from the beginning. They [the pilots] were, in fact, testing a new invention of lights on the propellers. One light was missing when I decided to shoot the photograph; the lights were uneven. I was, in fact, witnessing that this invention would not work. I took this shot and never shot again. Other lights had subsequently gone out because of the centrifugal force.

❧

WHATEVER SUBJECT YOU CHOOSE for this exercise, you should record it as objectively and as clearly as possible. The final image should get your message across at once, with no chance for confusion. While shooting a visual portrait of Egypt, Irina Ionesco came up with the idea of photographing a woman in such a way that she seemed to embody that country (opposite).

This photograph was very studied, like a sculpture, a vase. She is Egyptian, Cleopatra. She is the picture of femininity, prudence, her back turned. I had this idea because of her long hair and her Egyptian-like face. But all the more remarkable was that her shape was like that of an Egyptian vase. I was doing a study on Egypt at the time, and this to me was most definitely one way to show Egypt's splendor as a wonder.

NAVY HELICOPTER, 1949. © ANDREAS FEININGER.

FEMME ASSISE
EGYPTIENNE.
© IRINA IONESCO.

LIKE ANDREAS FEININGER, Angelo Lomeo faced an assignment that required him to definitively describe his subject. He explains that the most accurate way to capture the immensity of a rock quarry in Vermont was through contrast.

This photograph is of the largest granite quarries in the world. The juxtaposition with the man made the taking of this picture irresistible. I would have taken it without the man, but the presence of the man made it a special picture. I was on an assignment to portray the quarry. To me, this meant the juxtaposition of the quarry and the man. It was a man who cut the quarry. And it is a man who looks dwarfed by his quarry. He looks like an ant.

ROCK OF AGES GRANITE QUARRY, BARRE, VERMONT. © ANGELO LOMEO.

DIRECTING AN EXPLICIT ANALYSIS

IN THIS EXERCISE, YOUR GOAL is to explore the mechanical and technical advantages of your camera and films to reveal the most significant aspects of your subjects. Knowing your camera and different types of film intimately will help you produce better pictures. See what lengths you can go to, to define your subjects with the greatest precision. You should be able to explain every element and every detail included in the image, as well as why you employed specific techniques. What did you choose to have in focus and out of focus, and why? Why did you choose to illuminate either the foreground or the background? Why did you shoot in available light or, vice versa, why did you use a flash?

As you intellectually analyze your images, you'll see that certain techniques render your photographs more or less realistic or concrete. For example, using a closeup lens provides a potentially defining detail, such as the dugout at a baseball field. On the other hand, using a wide-angle lens at the field would produce a descriptive image, perhaps of the tension of a baseball player on the pitcher's mound surrounded by a large slice of the ballpark. Obviously, shooting with a closeup lens leads to more explicit pictures, while shooting with a wide-angle lens provides a context for the subject. This is just one of the many mechanical and technical choices you must make.

As you do this exercise, keep in mind that not only do you have the camera to consider, but also the negative, the positive, and photographic paper itself. You can utilize all of these factors in order to increase the clarity of your subject analyses. The added details must be rationally derived and intellectually employed to emphasize what you want to say via your photographs. The illogical or gratuitous manipulation of an image can weaken its impact. Aram Dervent describes how he went about creating a new photograph out of an old one (right). His goal was to make this image express the notion of censored thought. Through post-shooting manipulation, he succeeded in transforming this picture into a decisive means of communicating a precise message.

I took the original picture of a friend without knowing what I was going to do with it. This is a reconstruction, meaning that the photograph is merely the basic element, like wood, glass or stone, which permits me to construct a representation of censored thought. Thus, the eyes have the red band over them. The man is wearing a suit. I left the shirt and tie untouched since it makes him look like a statue. It is also an element which remains purely photographic.

The scratching of the negative in this case was to make him look like a bust of stone, the mouth atrophied, the body merely a support or means to support the final form. I also manipulated

the colors. This is superimposition of coloring with ink and tape on film, scratching of the negative, and burning with acid. I went to blue in the jacket because of its juxtaposition to the green and brown. The pale green tone works as the hardness of the stone.

You cannot forget the rapport of colors. The brown is at the bottom because I wanted to show oxidization, a phenomenon of the roll of film. After all, it is wood which is subject to aging, to other elements, and time. I knew I could not go any further. There would be no balance in the picture. Balance is a station, a frozen stop. If you go too far with scratching and acid, you can end up with ashes. There is a point of no return. Beyond that, the image is destroyed. There are harmonies that are clear to me, the same as in painting and music.

LES MONOLITHES, COSTUME CRAVATE, 1986. © ARAM DERVENT.

PHOTOGRAPHING LANDMARKS

FOR THIS EXERCISE, take a photograph of a place you aren't familiar with, as well as one of a place you're very familiar with. In each picture, make the location recognizable by highlighting landmarks or the layout so that a stranger would be able to identify it. Consider what you want to say about the spot and what the most effective way to do this is. For a photograph shot during the fall, Thierry Guinhut's goal was to unequivocably define a particular place (below).

The symbolism that I wanted was in my mind during the taking of this photograph, as well as carefully choosing when to take the photograph. I had already taken many photographs of the Marais Poitevin for my book, Le Marais Poitevin. This photograph reveals the marais in autumn. It is a moment which is necessary to reveal among others in a project which entails such a methodical approach to a region's geography.

I put the boat in the lower right to strengthen the composition and to underline the contrast of the mass of color on the moving surface, the softness of the lentils on the water tinted by the colored leaves. When I was taking this picture, I had the sensation of possessing a special synthetic-like place in the Marais Poitevin, the sensation of a balance and a formal precision. It is a sensation often sought after and only sometimes found, whether it be in landscape, water, or mountains even if it has to do with a precision other than geometrical. This photograph is more than capturing, but arranging and designing.

CONCHE COURDAULT. DUCULOT, PARIS. FROM *LE MARAIS POITEVIN*. © 1991 THIERRY GUINHUT.

As YOU SHOOT, you may decide that you want to add text to the photograph or series of images in order to make your observation all that much more explicit. There is no doubt as to the location of Bob Bishop's photograph. By including the area surrounding the fence, he captured a realistic representation of the subject.

The electrical power symbols on the posts of this gate are in fact the insignia of the ranch behind the gate. I was first taken by the blue of the fence and of the sky, a sky one sees only in the Southwest. In this context, the symbols on the posts took on their mythic symbol of power. It seemed to recall the Old West, all its power'and the guns. All of the Southwest's history and present seemed to be summed up in this framing of the fence, mountains, and sky. It is such a huge space and yet you cannot get in.

SANTA FE GATE. © BOB BISHOP.

WHEN PHOTOGRAPHING LANDMARKS, you don't always have to include the surrounding area for definition. A single, vertical closeup can be equally, or sometimes even more, succinct. This is the approach I took while shooting a new music center (below).

This photograph is a facet of the new philharmonic center in Naples, Florida. Had I taken a picture of the austere architecture with the surrounding palm trees, it could have been a photograph of a modern building in any southern clime. But this silver lady belongs uniquely to this Floridian city. Not only is she captured reflecting her context, but also within the confines of a vertical frame.

FOR THIS COMPELLING PHOTOGRAPH of a famous baseball field, Scott Mutter added artificial details (opposite). Although this sense of spatial relationships is right-brain-inspired, it is ultimately determined by the left hemisphere. He wanted to create an image that would effectively communicate his intellectually inspired message. The carefully calculated implementation of the additional elements resulted in a successful, left-brain-directed image.

As the controversy over installing lights at Wrigley Field entered its third year, I thought of a way to memorialize this phase of American and Chicago baseball history.

© KATHRYN MARX.

Creating an image that looked realistic would have meant taking sides, and if it turned out that the Cubs would play night games at home, then my image would be only a parody of the future. Thus, I decided to make an image of a game taking place during what appeared to be night, but under outrageous and impossible conditions.

The game photo I finally decided to use was from a day game played in 1987, roughly a year before the first night game at Wrigley. I chemically darkened the image, removing the daytime top and slipping in an actual, though altered, night skyline. Numerous other details were inserted or deleted for effect.

Clearly the most essential addition was the apparent source of light—flashlights held by the fans—which gives the image its qualities of humor, intrigue, and the beauty of a match-lighting event. In terms of the composition and interest, I wanted viewers to be close enough to the infield to feel that they were actually watching a play in progress, yet I wanted to capture enough of the fans in the stands to give the effect of human activity and implied motion all around.

FANS SHED LIGHT ON THE GAME. WRIGLEY FIELD, CHICAGO, 1987. FROM *SURRATIONAL IMAGES* (UNIVERSITY OF ILLINOIS PRESS). © 1987 SCOTT MUTTER.

DOCUMENTING A SEQUENCE

THIS EXERCISE CALLS FOR YOU to record a passage of time, short or long, via a series of photographs. You might, for example, decide to shoot pages from your journal or from a history book. Other options include highlighting one specific detail of evolution within a larger event and taking a "wide-angle" approach to a series of events, such as a weekend in Amsterdam or rush hour in Chicago. Once again, you may want to add text to the photographs, thereby making them all that much more concrete. You also need to decide whether black-and-white or color film better enables you to depict realistic objectivity. Nan Goldin chose color.

The first time I saw Cookie she was having a yard sale on her front porch in Provincetown. She was a cross between Tobacco Road and a Hollywood B-girl, the most fabulous woman I'd ever seen. Somebody told me she was the same Cookie from John Waters's movies. That summer, I kept meeting her at the bars, at parties, and at barbecues with her family: her girlfriend, Sharon;

COOKIE AT TIN PAN ALLEY, NYC 1983. © NAN GOLDIN.

her son, Max; and her dog, Beauty. Part of how we got close was through me photographing her—the photos were intimate and then we were. I was outside of her, and taking her picture let me in.

Cookie was a social light, a beauty, my idol. Over the years, she became a writer, a critic, my best friend, my family. We lived through the peaks and the dread together in Provincetown, New York, New Orleans, Baltimore, Positano.

While I was away in 1988, Cookie got sick. When I came back to see her in August 1989, the effects of AIDS had robbed her of her ability to talk. But when I photographed her, she spoke to me; she was as present as ever.

On September 14th her husband, Vittorio Scarpati, died from an AIDS-related illness, and after that Cookie kind of gave up. She died on November 10th in the hospice of Cabrini Medical Center.

I used to think I couldn't lose anyone if I photographed them enough. I put together this series of pictures of Cookie from over the 13 years I knew her in order to keep her with me. In fact it shows me how much I've lost.

COOKIE IN THE GARDEN AT CIRO'S, PROVINCETOWN, MA, SEPTEMBER, 1989. © NAN GOLDIN.

PHOTOGRAPHING A RELATIONSHIP

HERE, YOUR TASK IS to record the evolution of a relationship with a series of photographs or one historically concrete photograph. The picture or pictures should explain, without room for any conjecture on the part of the viewers, what you want to document about the relationship. No metaphorical images are allowed here, only pictures that reveal specific events or interactions. What you want to show should be as clear to you as it was to Sonja Bullaty (below).

I wanted to do justice to Edinburgh as well as photography. All of these elements with these two people meeting could come together only in photography because it was a chance moment. It worked in balance of color and design at the moment that I shot! I had to shoot it at that moment or not at all. The entire image is about brief encounters in every sense.

WHILE SONJA BULLATY'S INTENTION was to capture an impromptu meeting in a single image, Araki Nobuyoshi's extensive quest was to unveil his day-to-day life in a series of shots (opposite). His sense of realism went so far as to include his camera in even the most mundane activities.

I have related my daily life in the form of a journal illustrated by the series of photographs. Even on the table of my dining room, next to the salt and pepper, the camera is there, which permits me to shoot without interruption before, during, and after the meals. All my photographs are taken with an ordinary camera without a flash and a system which dates the shots.

Of course the journal, entitled "A Sentimental Journey," is as complex as any journal, any novel. However, the method of putting together this collection of images was based on daily taking of photographs of my life with my wife and our world.

BRIEF ENCOUNTER (EDINBURGH, SCOTLAND). © SONJA BULLATY.

GIRL ASLEEP IN BOAT. FROM THE "SENTIMENTAL JOURNEY" SERIES. © NOBUYOSHI ARAKI.

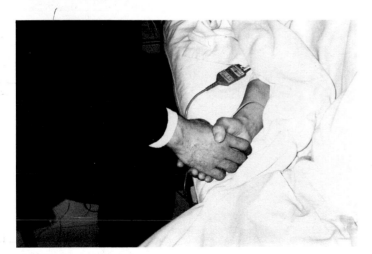

HAND IN HAND. FROM THE "SENTIMENTAL JOURNEY" SERIES.
© NOBUYOSHI ARAKI.

GIRL IN TRAIN. FROM THE "SENTIMENTAL JOURNEY" SERIES.
© NOBUYOSHI ARAKI.

PHOTOGRAPHING A RESOLUTION

FOR THIS EXERCISE, PHOTOGRAPH a decision or a resolution of a situation. The picture should depict a definitive moment in someone's life; this can be any situation that shows a coming to terms with reality. Before looking around for a possible source for this photograph, think about what precisely you're looking for. You might, for example, want to pretend that you are on assignment and must photograph a tennis player winning a Grand Slam championship or a jockey losing a race. This shouldn't be an image that suddenly appears before you, which you attach a resolution to later. Duane Michals is a proponent of this method, and his pictures prove that previsualization can lead to strongly directed photographs (below).

My work is premeditated. I figure things out carefully. There is no wasted motion. My work is very calculated. I don't wait for the muses to whisper. In "Grandpa Goes to Heaven," I didn't wander into a room and let it happen. Many changes happen, but they happen in my brain. And I think out changes and possibilities before I take the picture. The hard part is done, so that taking the picture is the easy part. Taking the picture is just the tip of the iceberg.

As YOU PREPARE TO DO this exercise, keep in mind that it requires premeditated, intellectual deduction. Your purpose here is to create a sequence that you've directed and that objectively expresses your analysis. The idea should be completely broken down in your mind before you shoot, not afterward. Larry Clark made a harrowing portrait that was carefully planned in advance (opposite).

I needed a new way to work that was not documentary. I wanted to see if I could work in my studio and be satisfied with the results. So I asked people to come to the studio. And then I met this kid. He had a jean jacket with heavy-metal stuff. He came over, and I was going to make an environment in the studio like his room would be. I found posters that I liked and that would probably be in his room, and I put them on the wall.

At the same point, I pulled out the gun as a prop to give him something to play around with. Then he spontaneously put it in his mouth. Earlier, a friend had said that if he got AIDS, he would buy a Bijan pistol for $10,000 and shoot himself. I knew of an AIDS benefit show that was coming up, so I took this shot for that show. The benefit exhibition was in the back of my mind throughout this shoot.

FROM THE "GRANDPA" SERIES. © DUANE MICHALS.

© LARRY CLARK.

95

PROGRAMMING A PHOTOGRAPH

THIS LEFT-BRAIN EXERCISE calls for you to summon your intellectual strength and stamina for accuracy. You need your most directed sense of straightforward visual convergence or logical unity in order to put together a picture. The emphasis here is on tight composition; a rational integration of the elements in the picture will communicate the strongest message. You can do this in a number of ways. You can cut and unite various photographs that you've already taken, merge negatives, superimpose one slide over another, or simply arrange a selection of images in succession. You can also combine images on a computer, as Frank Horvat did (below). Whatever method you decide on, be sure to base the composition on an explicit analysis of what you want to say.

No matter how much you rely on feeling, you have to possess and use good technique. When I work on the computer, the main part of the work consists of fitting together fractions from different images. On the screen is the puzzle which I am putting together. It takes some time, but at some point, a combination seems to click.

Sometimes it happens by accident. Computer accidents do happen. But this "click" is straightforward composition and balance according to everything that the academy says makes a good reportage picture—except that in this case, the decisive moment is not only the moment of the shooting but the moment of composing. It is still all of the mechanisms that make a good picture: composition and balance according to the Cartier-Bresson and Magnum school, except without the reportage ingredients.

MYTHOLOGIES. PSYCHE. © FRANK HORVAT.

BOB BISHOP ALSO USED the latest technology in order to "program" a photograph (below). He thought that the applications offered by a computer would most readily enable him to realize his goal. He explains the necessity of keeping the intended image in mind as you work.

I had to take time to master the machines, all of the programs, how many dots per inch, for example, so that the image appears photographic when it is printed. I am exploring new kinds of technology, and it is very easy to get diverted. What I am looking for is to transform images. I took this shot three years ago. Coming from my many years' stay in Europe and seeing the cold-drink cup, I thought it seemed perfect for my study of "American Icons, Route 66." I put the cup against a white table top because I wanted it highlighted, to be the most graphic possible. I saw this

photograph being done graphically from the beginning, but from the beginning there was something missing.

I tried traditional techniques to alter the image. I like simple backgrounds, so there were many possibilities. But by scanning the image, I could finally transform it into the image that I really wanted in the first place. But I can spend days changing the colors or details. What I finally decided upon corresponded to what I saw in the photograph when I shot it, the color, the contrast, the hard graphic quality.

I had previsualized what I wanted when I approached the computer. This was to show the new international culture, what society has become. The design, form, and shape with a graphic message, the digitalization of the image, had added that dimension to it explicitly.

COLD DRINK. © BOB BISHOP.

PHOTOGRAPHING PEOPLE OBJECTIVELY

TAKE A PHOTOGRAPH OF YOURSELF or someone else that you feel shows yourself or your subject as objectively as possible. In other words, the subject should be recognizable. Once you've mastered this, challenge the left side of your mind even further. Attempt to reveal emotion with your eye directed toward a straightforward, concrete analysis. You may want to start with photographing your own feelings as literally as possible. For example, compose your face so that it expresses fear, and photograph it.

As you work, remember that emotions are rarely logical and certainly aren't "felt" objectively. However, you must challenge yourself to find the image that best communicates the emotion in question so that viewers who are unaware of your goal recognize which feeling you hope to capture. Whether the most descriptive images of individuals show their feelings or characteristic gestures, you can conclusively capture the essence of their personality with the help of your left brain. Martha Swope's images of ballet dancers reveal the value of putting yourself aside in order to punctuate the uniqueness of your subject.

A photograph is best when someone says, "That really is Zorba or that really is Colleen Dewhurst." I would much rather they say that than, "That is a Martha Swope photograph." It's perfectly valid to look at a photograph by Richard Avedon and say, "That is an Avedon." But I have a different approach.

☙

FINALLY, AS YOU DO THIS EXERCISE, see whether color film or black-and-white film adds a greater measure of reality or objectivity to the portrait. Black-and-white photography has the tradition of documentation behind it, yet the world exists in color.

MIKHAIL BARYSHNIKOV IN
"PUSH COMES TO SHOVE."
© 1990 MARTHA SWOPE.

EDWARD VILLELLA IN "PRODIGAL SON." © 1990 MARTHA SWOPE.

CREATING A BOOK-COVER IMAGE

HERE, YOUR TASK IS TO MAKE a photograph for a book cover. First, choose a book and read it. As you go through it, keep in mind that the photograph should integrate the most significant aspects of the book; these convey what the book is about or based upon. Your left brain's sense of the historical and the deductively analytical will help you select what is most pertinent for your expository picture. Gear the details for this precise delineation toward conveying the book's contents as succinctly as possible.

Although the book cover must be informative, it must also be appealing. Remember, a book jacket is supposed to attract the book-buying public. As such, your goal is twofold, and the choice of elements is all the more critical. Again, check to see which type of film best suits your subject, black-and-white or color.

Patrick Boucher was given very specific instructions when he was hired to shoot a book-cover image; he was told to photograph a boy of a certain age who had a hard life after World War II (below). Because Boucher had a sense of Paris after the war, through both research and personal experience, he was able to find an appropriate subject and setting.

I was asked to shoot a photograph for a story based on the life of the author, an unhappy boy after the war, living with great difficulties. His parents were immigrants who worked very hard.

I chose these colors to reconstitute the period after the war in old Paris, its old houses and old streets. This is the story of a clever and sensitive boy, so I looked to give him a special look in his eye. It was necessary to show the boy's face with the hardships of life as well. The editors asked for a photograph which would represent the author at the age of 10, alone in Paris after the war.

L'OEIL DU LAPIN.
© 1989 PATRICK
BOUCHER.

100

PHOTOGRAPHING YOUR SENSE OF HUMOR

TAKE A PHOTOGRAPH of your sense of humor. In other words, you must tell a joke visually. You must make it work for the most literal-minded person, which is you while you're doing this exercise. You may find a single shot that, in all its deductive rationality, is logically funny. The juxtaposition of elements may be responsible for rendering the image amusing or laughable. The joke may also take the form of a written text that you add to the picture. Your job is to make people, and yourself, laugh. As Angelo Lomeo explains, you know that you've hit upon a humorous photograph when the image makes you laugh first (below).

I saw the stop sign and the cloud right above it. I knew that I had to have it. It was too funny to resist. When I finally found the right angle, *I took the shot without a moment's hesitation. A bit of humor never hurts. This is a picture that doesn't need words. It is purely humor. Some photographers make this kind of photograph with doubles or other kinds of manipulation, but this one was done on the spot.*

೧

ONCE YOU'VE COMPLETED these diverse exercises, the muscle of your left brain should be pretty well flexed. Perhaps you'll find yourself thinking more logically more of the time, both when you photograph and when you're involved in your daily activities. Regardless, awareness of your left-brain potential is the most important benefit. A greater number of possible straightforward approaches to your photography will now be at your disposal. And the application of them is simply a matter or practice, desire, and necessity.

ARROW AND CLOUD, TEXAS. © ANGELO LOMEO.

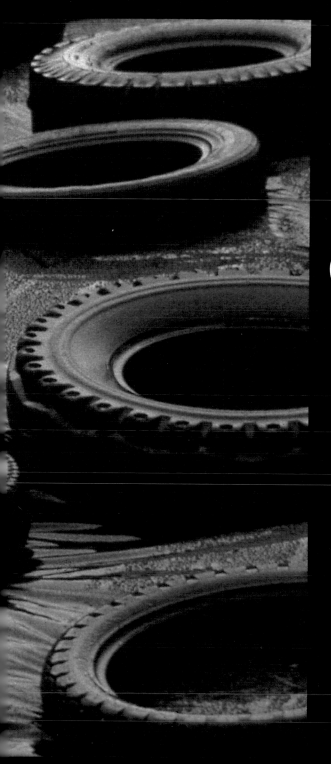

PART 3

RIGHT BRAIN/LEFT BRAIN COMBINATIONS

UNITING INTELLECT AND INTUITION

WHILE ALL PHOTOGRAPHS REQUIRE the participation of both sides of the brain, many images show a dominating influence of one side, so much so that the other hemisphere's tendencies aren't visible. But some photographs reveal a more balanced perspective, and sometimes others even reflect equal input from the two sides of the brain. A picture created with equal force from the right and the left brain might be impulsively conceptualized on the spot and its details photographed; the image is then assembled under the direction of left-brain convergence.

As I discuss in the first section of this book, some photographs are inspired by a deeply intuitive sense of the subject, which is born in the right brain. The second section focuses on images that the analytical left brain designs and effects. This section explores images that are combinations of right- and left-brain functions. In pictures like that of Béatrice Helg, the work begins with an intellectual concept that is developed intuitively by the right brain and executed by the left brain until a subjective sense of balance is achieved (below).

Each photograph is the result of a long process involving both intellect and intuition, which, in fact, are interacting with each other to go farther in their exploration. When creating a picture, I begin with a rather definite concept and preconceived structure in mind. The first step of the construction is primarily an intellectual exercise. Then, little by little, I intuitively add or subtract objects, touches of color, and create the lighting. My analytical reasoning comes back into play, examining the space in formation (the coherence, the tension as well as balance between the different elements) and studying the image's frame. When I sense a unity between my feelings and intentions, the world I have been creating is complete.

Although my images are highly constructed, they are photographs of open spaces, which can continue their evolution, their transformation under the spectator's eye. Depending on whether the viewer approaches them with his intellect only, or whether he also lets his imagination and sensitivity come into play, his own inner experience of the pictures will be completely different.

THÉATRES DE LA LUMIERE VI," 1991.
CIBACHROME PRINT, 35³/₈ × 31¹/₈ INCHES.
COURTESY OF THE JAYNE H. BAUM
GALLERY, NEW YORK. © BÉATRICE HELG.

WHILE IT IS IMPOSSIBLE to tap the left and right hemispheres of the brain simultaneously, some pictures are the result of a highly integrated effort from both points of view. As a result, the left- and right-brain contributions are equally apparent. For example, Joel-Peter Witkin had a clear-cut idea of what he wished to reveal through two of his images, but his analytical left brain didn't entirely govern how he manipulated them. While he made "Woman Once a Bird," there ultimately came a moment when the meditation on the woman's relationship with life satisfied his sense of completion (below right). Here, Witkin is not only telling a story but also revealing a deep sense of the fallen angel within everyone, including viewers and himself.

This photograph shows the real and the applied without exposing those boundaries. The image is also a meditation on a real person's relationship with life. Her "being" is her fetishism. She is not the romantic plaything of Man Ray's "Le Violin d'Ange." She is ourselves as a fallen angel. Fallen, when we dimly sense that our real world extends from the earth to a place of sublime bliss, instead of the emptiness and fear we all share.

౮

"LAS MENINAS," another photograph made by Witkin, was commissioned by the Ministry of Culture of Spain (below left). Although he was shooting an assignment and had guidelines to follow, he managed to leave his stamp on the final image. Furthermore, each element has a reason for being there. There is nothing gratuitous.

It was an opportunity for me to make a photograph based on a Spanish masterwork. I chose the work of Velazquez since it doesn't present a narrative. My interpretation would contain clues to my own intentions. The small princess is a richly decorated, functionless object, representing the slavery of the people of Spain. The projector to her left signifies the possibility of the use of the "camera obscura" by Velazquez. There are many more signifiers existing here representing historical connectives. But the essence of this image is that we all are born, live, and die in isolation—that the need to love is really the great narrative of all human life.

౮

WITKIN'S PERSONAL VISION is evident throughout "Las Meninas." All photographers—in fact, all individuals—have a unique perspective on or point of view regarding the world. People are arrested to some degree by their limited sense of the notion of reality. However, with some effort, they can expand the limits of their subjectivity through various forms of manipulation. As an individual, you can become more informed. As a photographer, you can manipulate an image to reflect a new realization when you come upon a truth.

LAS MENINAS, NEW MEXICO, 1987. COURTESY OF THE PACE MCGILL GALLERY, NEW YORK CITY, AND THE FRAENKEL GALLERY, SAN FRANCISCO. © JOEL-PETER WITKIN.

WOMAN ONCE A BIRD, LOS ANGELES, 1990. COURTESY OF THE PACE MCGILL GALLERY, NEW YORK CITY, AND THE FRAENKEL GALLERY, SAN FRANCISCO. © JOEL-PETER WITKIN.

PHOTOGRAPHIC MANIPULATION

ANOTHER WAY TO RELEASE and mix left- and right-brain potentials is to mix photography with another medium. Of course, there are simpler methods of photographic manipulation. You can determine the final look of arrangement of your images yourself, or you can allow someone else to manipulate them. For a series of images, Gilles Maury determined the contents by analyzing symbols and studying the technical photographic process (below). The metaphorical side of Maury's work is expressed by his willingness to allow the curator of an exhibition to determine the order in which the images will appear.

This series of 10 photographs, in fact, silver emulsion on glass, is a funeral motif. It is based on people and things which existed before me and will be there long after me. The elements are associated in their order in the place of exhibition. One image is of an oil lamp, symbolizing life which is not eternal but when it is lit, it glows. It shows itself like the life or a souvenir of that life, like a photograph.

If you take a photograph, it is a fraction of time, a commemorative of the past. In the end, it does not matter in which order they are placed since it is a group. That is what is important. They are arranged on the floor as a whole.

OIL LAMP (NOIR ET BLANC, DIAPO). © GILLES MAURY.

THE MOMENT OF CONNECTION

SOME PHOTOGRAPHERS KNOW that they're strongly drawn to a particular place or subject without intellectually understanding why until after they photograph the subject for a while. Other photographers approach a subject with one specific intention and successfully execute something else entirely. Mark Klett found a great deal more than he expected when he visited Utah (below). He describes what he discovered while photographing this area. He wanted to avoid shooting an overly expository image of the scene. Klett's message combines the sadness he felt while looking at the landscape and his metaphorical side, which was initially attracted to the curves of the tire tracks.

This terrain was incredibly desolate. It was like being on the moon. It was not like sending yourself to a new planet, however, but more like a place people had left. The tracks were the first thing to catch my eye, the gracefulness of the loops. I realized that they don't last too long and that there was nothing on that land that the vehicles that had caused the tracks could kill anyway.

Behind me was a well-known formation called Factory Butte where a lot of people come to shoot. But already I had seen that it was not such a pristine landscape anymore. It was incredibly desolate yet distressed in that every piece of ground had already been stamped on. The title of the photograph, "Weekend Explorers," shows the irony involved.

I saw the graceful lines of the tracks, but at the same time their destructive force. Here was this classic landscape with this modernity on top of it which had a certain feeling of pathos to it, a feeling of sadness. This is not just a picture saying, "Look how awful this is." I wanted to avoid that, in fact, and keep the feeling of identity there with its sadness. In keeping the gracefulness of the loops, I tried to make a picture of the irony of the situation without being didactic, without giving a lecture or making the image alien or off-putting. My photographs never work if I force something. But if I am really feeling something, the shot comes from the bottom up.

TRAILS OF WEEKEND EXPLORERS, HANKSVILLE, UTAH, 4/18/91. © MARK KLETT.

ALTHOUGH IT SOUNDS CONTRADICTORY, an imaginative look at an object can render its reality much more accessible and appealing to people who rely on photographers to create a more attractive reality. This reality is, in essence, a fantasy. For example, when shooting fashion, Franco Fontana can direct his imagination to construct a picture that is based on reality but is approaching the realm of surrealism. His left-brain talents are the first to be summoned; he carefully thinks an approach through and then delineates the specifics of the shot. In this way, he can rely on his spontaneous imagination at critical moments during the shoot.

When I am working on fashion, I always work with a creative approach, in a way of giving original and personal results. Consequently, the process of realization is very similar to when I do landscape photographs or other subjects. For fashion, the project is born first in my head, but the realization always has its part of spontaneity.

In the world we discover only what we have inside ourselves. It is a game between what you imagine and what you see. And it is always what you imagine that you photograph. But it is necessary for the external world to see and discover what it is that you imagine.

ↀ

WHEN YOU PLAN WHAT you're going to photograph, leave yourself more room for spontaneity than you might think necessary. Don't restrict yourself to a formal adherence to technique. Human nature seems to dictate that people feel freer when they must act within well-defined boundaries than when they have no guidelines to follow. Once they know their parameters, they seem almost fearlessly willing to let themselves go from within. When people have no limits, they tend to look for them rather than exploring all possibilities. Doing this exercise should prevent you from falling into this trap. Seize the moment of connection.

FOR VALENTINO IN *VOGUE* USA. © 1988 FRANCO FONTANA.

FOR VERSACE.
© FRANCO FONTANA.

DOCUMENTING REALITY

SOLID REPORTAGE PHOTOGRAPHY combines the demands of intellectual insight and formal support. As Stephen Shames makes apparent, this kind of work requires your intuition to be immediately accessible under even the most grueling circumstances. In addition, your intellect must be razor sharp in such shooting situations.

I consider myself both a journalist and an artist. Journalistic photography is based on "reality" in the same manner as a documentary film. You are saying this is an unbiased observation rather than being something made up or composed. This goal of objectivity pulls one way, but for me, reality is also an individual's psychological perspective and dreams. The unconscious mind contains as much reality as the "facts" of the conscious world. And, in fact, our unconscious desires influence public events. So this is relevant to journalism, although it is discouraged by our traditional, two-dimensional, "just-the-facts" approach.

When I take a photograph for a story, I try to go for both realities (inner and outer). My feelings go into my pictures. Reality is what we feel about it, not just what we see on the surface.

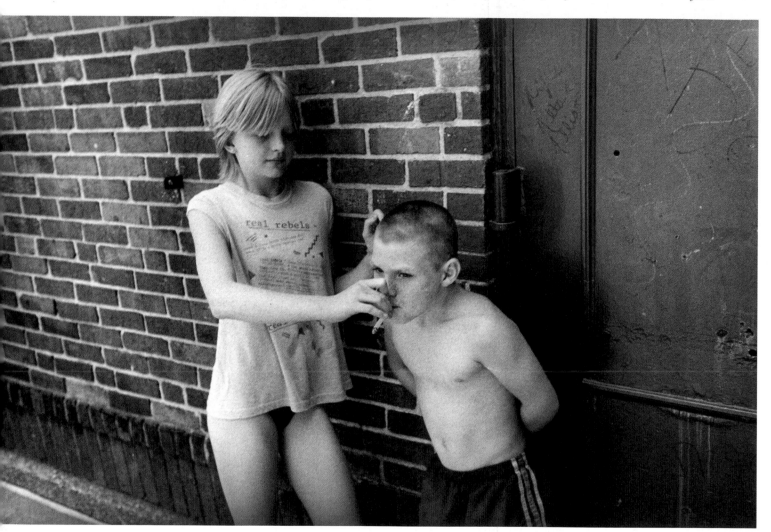

CIGARETTE. FROM *OUTSIDE THE DREAM.* © 1991 STEPHEN SHAMES.

I like pictures that have emotion to them, rather than a two-dimensional news photo. That is why I do stories rather than news pictures. The flow of the photographs gives more opportunity for depth and emotion. I want to evoke deep emotions in the viewer—to reach his or her unconscious mind. Good photographs get beyond rationality to that visual, dream-like state that is the core of our emotions.

These photographs from my book, Outside the Dream, have to do with poverty. They deal with issues of survival, violence, family, and love. These are among my favorite images from the book. They all haunt me.

I plan my photographs carefully, but the planning takes place before I ever take out the camera. I consciously put myself in places where particular situations exist and might happen in front of my camera. However, when I get there, it is no longer on such a rational level. I like to be very loose. I don't plan my pictures. I let myself go. I use the real world as my text but my unconscious as my guide.

MAX KISSES VANESSA. FROM *OUTSIDE THE DREAM*. © 1991 STEPHEN SHAMES.

SIMILARLY, LAURENCE BRUN'S PRIMARY GOAL was to shoot informative photographs . However, she found that she must be open to what might unexpectedly appear before the viewfinder. Like Shames, she learned not to suceumb to the restrictions of a "just-the-facts" approach. She also discovered that an assignment can serve as a helpful support or framework rather than as an inhibitor.

But so-called documentary photography risks being overlooked by an inquiring public if its form doesn't drive the picture into the eyes and hearts of viewers. So reportage photographers, whose top priority is to record with their film, may sometimes seem to put the aesthetic framing of their pictures second. In fact, however, composing effectively must be second nature.

It is an old piece of wisdom that the left-brain-determined contents of an image work best when the holistic, right-brain-guided form is equally strong. As such, the most effective reportage photographs are those images that are emphasized by their contents, focal point, framing, and cropping. While this guideline pertains to the work of all photographers, reportage photographers often have the added obligation of fulfilling this left- and right-brain combination while making a split-second decision and operating their camera. Brun explains the difference between getting informative pictures and getting something more.

I wanted to show how this woman works, the hardship of her work, her perseverance, and her suffering. I was in Afghanistan to reveal the life of the Afghanistan women with a sociological approach to their environment, their traditions, their lives. As a documentary photographer, my goal was to show what she does, transporting the grain in the mountains. I had the added information in her facial expression. But I could not just take the picture; I had to wait for the best moment, when the way she was framed by her environment would add impact to the photograph.

A photographer has to remember harmony in a photograph. You learn the techniques for accomplishing this in school, and then after school, you forget them. It is not that any of it is forgotten, but merely becomes internalized in the work so that they come out spontaneously. For me, the best moment to photograph this woman was when her movement corresponded with the diagonals of the mountains behind her.

At the same time that I was taking this photograph, I did not know literally why I felt she was best captured at the moment which I shot. But afterward, I could see how her leg was situated with the diagonal that descends from the mountains behind her, her foot in the same direction and the sack which also underlines her movement. It is another sense, a composition of diagonals. But this came from my instinctive sight. For although I had the subject clearly before my eyes, this aesthetic instinct was the mechanism which put my finger down on the shutter-release button at that precise moment.

DAILY LIFE OF A "NURISTANI" WOMAN—AFGHANISTAN 1972. © LAURENCE BRUN.

WHILE TAKING ANOTHER informative photograph in Afghanistan, Brun was most moved by the hands holding the dough. Within the context of her goal to shoot documentary photographs, her intuition placed these objects at the image's point of punctuation. Brun's right-brain sensitivity provided the strength of this picture, and the information it contains is underlined by this point of concern.

My first concern when I took this photograph was documentary. But the gesture of her hands, for me, was something sacred. It is a spiritual element in the photograph, the way she is holding the ball of dough. There is something archaic, primitive that talks of a custom in 1970, the earth, the nourishment. These people and the elements are primitive.

The bread is the center of the photograph. I chose this photograph from my contact sheet because it is the most harmonious. There is a unity of circles and triangles. At the point of the center triangle is the ball of dough, the "Punctom" as Roland Barthes explains in his book La Chambre Claire. *It is the detail in the picture which attracts the eye.*

I have always had this aesthetic concern in spite of my first priority being documentary. When it is a good photograph, it will go deeper and hit a vibration in the viewer, as well as in me when I look at the photograph again long after I have taken it or experienced its factual details. There should always be a spiritual aspect within its unity.

"HAZARA" WOMEN MAKING
BREAD—AFGHANISTAN 1972.
© LAURENCE BRUN.

REPORTAGE PHOTOGRAPHY IS UNIQUE because it is based on the specificity of a decisive moment. If you don't shoot at that precise moment in time, you may miss the peak of an event rather than freeze it forever. A split-second decision determines whether you capture a situation, as well as how well you capture it. You've already thought about your subject and know the reason why you've placed yourself in a particular situation. But once you are there, you must try to empty your mind of all thought in order for you to be completely in the moment and receptive to your intuition and your surroundings. Simply react to them with uncluttered clarity. Sebastiao Salgado reveals how this approach enables him to shoot his compelling photographs.

When I did the series of photographs on my cherished Latin America, it lasted seven years, but also seven centuries since I seemed to go back in time. I merely participated in the unraveling of time and events at a speed which is both slow and dense, which marks the passage of all of the eras in this region of the world.

I dreamt of this enchanted continent and of all of its fantasy, inherent in a land of incredible history. I let my imagination run across the immense green mountains and blood. I also crossed unfinished wars of legendary peasants and miners like revolutionary ghosts. I was dreaming that I walked among the indescribable

mysticism of sertao among men armored in leather, crossed their desperate struggles to survive in this place which is so arid, so poor, and yet with a strong morale throughout the country.

I dreamt of the Sierra Madre, its mists, its hallucinogenic mushrooms and peyote, its deaths so alive in the imagination of everybody. There it is really difficult to know if we are an integral part of the world or another since death is an inseparable sister of daily life. Armed with the arsenal of so many chimeras, I decided to plunge into the most concrete of this unreal universe of Latin America, so mysterious, suffering, heroic, and full of nobility. There comes a moment when it is no longer you who takes the photograph, but receives the way to do it quite naturally and fully.

❦

THE RICHNESS OF SALGADO'S WORK lies not only in the facts of life that it reveals, but also in the underlying realities. The moment he chooses to press the shutter-release button, he goes beyond maximizing the documentation to a deep-seated, timeless intuition regarding his subjects' feelings. While Salgado's photographs portray historical, concrete realism, they also make viewers come face to face with the full impact of his oneness with what he sees.

PHOTOGRAPHS © SEBASTIAO SALGADO.

BREAKING THE RULES

WHEN YOUR LEFT- AND RIGHT-BRAIN impulses work with equally strong input, the result can be well-structured photography, even visual poetry. This form of expression comes from a carefully collected and then released energy that is free to roam within a spontaneously determined order. To create striking images, Gerd Bonfert works within the limitless "confines" of his body and photographic techniques (below). His left brain affords him a great deal of liberty as he spontaneously makes images of his body correspond to his introspective analyses. The precision of his abstractions serves to enhance the ironies and dichotomies of his insights.

From the beginning, I have used my body for the purpose of my investigation of the photographic process. Photography is an excellent medium for freezing a precise moment. But the body is merely the appearance of our inner world, what we give of ourselves to the rest of the world and which can take the shape of endless representations. Sometimes I show the body X-rayed by overpowerful flashes of light, turned into luminous and curvy courses, the body set afire like a torch conveying the uncontrolled strength which burns within our most intimate feelings. I am more and more wary of the slow process of creation which turns the real into images. The eyes, the privileged organs for discovering the outside world, turn themselves inward toward the self, thus forming a cycle where the retinal vision is suppressed to the advantage of an interior vision into darkness.

COURTESY OF THE GALERIE BOUQUERET + LEBON, PARIS. © GERD BONFERT.

DIETER APPELT ALSO PHOTOGRAPHS himself a great deal (below). This gives him the freedom to exercise his well-thought-out approach with lengthy exposures. When he shoots, he lets go of all left-brain-generated inhibitions, such as any intellectual self-consciousness. As a result, successive pictures of Appelt don't reflect the left brain's tendencies to work sequentially or to pay any attention to details of exposure; they simply open his viewers' eyes to a way of seeing that is far removed from any notion of logic. Appelt lets his audience into a world drenched in metaph or and substantiated illusion.

My approach is careful. I use a long time exposure so that each shot passes by a poetic energy, and that makes its impression the knowledge of details and fragments. But I do not like to establish rules, especially when a ditch separates, in general, the first idea and the final result.

The pleasure of photography must still furnish explanations about my camera and my way of working. I refuse to use possibilities offered by the new sophisticated techniques, especially in this area. I can seize the essence of the sensitive world, show how some realities escape a superficial observer, suffer a mutation. I can show how this observer creates a mental universe made of balance and receptivity.

In the more than 400 successive photographs which I have taken of myself, I have been able to put into form the material within photography. In furthering my investigations, I am looking to transfer the invisible into images.

I have disinterested myself from registering the moment in order to approach the essence of reality, its intrinsic nature and invisibility. My photographs do not address reason but a magic reality. In my research of the body, I engage in the unity of the consciousness of life, of the being and the body.

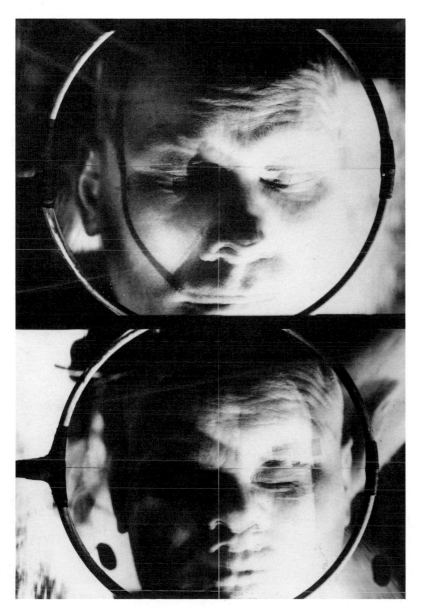

CANTO. COURTESY OF THE GALERIE BOUQUERET + LEBON, PARIS. © DIETER APPELT.

WHEN BOTH HEMISPHERES of your mind are being tapped, you sometimes rationally follow steps to a point of spontaneously taking off. You are free to wander within self-made boundaries of regulation. And as you shoot, you may find that the technical aspect of photography itself can be a jolt in a new direction into unfamiliar territory, guided by your left brain. In this foreign land of possibilities, only the right brain's intuition can lead you around. At this juncture, you may rediscover that rules are meant to be broken. This orderly process is evident in Arthur Tress's images (below).

As I was working on "Fish Tank Sonata," I became aware of a curious phenomenon. The still-life objects which protruded from the aquarium were visually broken at the surface. As the light moves from air to water, it is refracted, or bent, while it travels from one medium of optical density to another at different speeds according to the laws of physics.

This illusionist jump from one parallel force field to another surface could be seen as a metaphor for the challenge to the contemporary eye as it is dislodged from its conventional habits of visual response by the extreme violence of contemporary life. The photographic image-maker must move from his nineteenth-century role as a mere recorder of reality into the realm of transposed allegorical imagination to meet the new demands of simultaneous communication throughout the universe. Pushed into this new status as inventor of potent symbols by the infinite manipulative possibilities of the computer-generated digital print, the photographer, to stay on top and ahead of this overwhelming technology, must retrain his mind, not his lens, to be the source of analytical and creative expression.

He must use his total mental facilities to bridge the most complex intellectual concepts of our time and their unique graphic equivalents. His hyperaware intelligence must shatter the old clichés of the accepted pictorial vernacular to construct a stimulating, fresh language resonant with the augmented capacities of the modern eye. It is only within the expanding brain and not the latest optical or microprocessing equipment that the tools will be fabricated.

❧

HERE, TRESS SPEAKS OF an exciting role for photographers that many forget. Not only do they have a new means for capturing images, but also they're slowly being accepted into the art world's mainstream as a potential source of innovative imagery. However, rather than relying exclusively on promising new technology, they must also look inward to their imaginative right brain.

FIRST EXPERIMENTS. © ARTHUR TRESS.

DANCE FOR THE CHAOS,
DANCE FOR THE ORDER,
FEEL JUBILATION
HERE BY THE WATER.
NEW YORK, 1989

FROM *FISH TANK SONATA*. © ARTHUR TRESS.

118

SOME PHOTOGRAPHERS FIND untapped reserves of inspiration with jolts from new methods of image-making. Exciting progress in color-film technology has enabled some photographers to take giant steps in both their development and careers. Other photographers, however, prefer to remain within the spectrum of black-and-white work. They feel that when they shoot in black and white, their imaginations are free to utilize all the inherent subtleties and nuances.

Putting refined craftsmanship at the disposal of a finely tuned intuitive sense leads to a highly successful combination. This is the best of both worlds because each skill enhances the potential of the other. Although Frances Murray's work focuses on a full range of emotions, her left-brain talents keep her in control (below and overleaf). Since she is the director, producer, and subject of her photographs, she enjoys complete freedom.

The source of Murray's prose, which is created apart from the related images, reflects both metaphorical and timeless thoughts. Murray carefully photographs and frames various emotions and then purposefully aligns free-flowing prose with the corresponding image. The writing emphasizes its content or tone. This unusual combination is a strongly unified effort; the right- and left-brain impulses keep each other in check.

I have been photographing myself for as long as I have been a photographer, 15 years. Self-portraits allow me to reveal a wide range of emotions and provide a forum to express my deepest personal thoughts, fears, and anxieties. Making a self-portrait is very comfortable for me since I am in complete control. Nobody else is required, and I like the freedom it provides. As I photograph, I allow the constraints of my ordered routine to drop away and open myself to imagery that delves into the realms of my psyche.

The ability to depart from the ordinary and enter into the unknown, the questionable, is a major factor in all my work. I am secretive by nature and don't easily share my feelings, so this process is almost a necessary balancing aspect of my life. In the privacy of my studio, I can reveal to the camera this full spectrum of my emotions.

Writing the prose parallels my need to photograph. It isn't anything I set out to do. It just happened. As I photographed, I wrote, but I did not consciously write a specific text for a specific photograph. Rather, once the photographs were processed, I would then read over the text I had written and determine how certain pieces would speak to and extend the "tone" of the photographic image.

✧

THE PHOTOGRAPHS IN THIS SECTION were prompted initially by either the right or left brain and then executed by the other hemisphere. Perhaps you'll decide to shoot a series of photographs of a particular telephone booth during the day. If you then have an impulse to put the first five images together or to colorize them, don't look upon this as an interruption. Follow the impulse—it may be right on target, just unexpected.

With the burgeoning photographic technology, there is a new spectrum of potential left-brain ingenuity. However, when you exploit these advances to their fullest, you might find that its metaphorical or poetic applications actually enable you to fulfill needs that previously went unsatisfied. Although this technology will help you create images, don't let it mislead or deceive you. The most logical and often productive decision you can make is to follow your impulses.

SELF-PORTRAIT: REMOTENESS.
© FRANCES MURRAY.

SELF-PORTRAIT: ANXIETY. © FRANCES MURRAY.

TIME. WE ALL WORRY ABOUT IT.
WHERE HAS IT GONE? MY SENSE
OF SMELL AND QUICK ABILITY TO
FANTASIZE EASILY TRANSPORT ME
FROM THE MUNDANE, PROPELLING
ME INTO FANTASY. WHEN I RETURN
RELUCTANTLY AND GLIMPSE MY
REFLECTION IN THE MIRROR, I
WONDER, WHO IS THIS STRANGER
STARING OUT AT ME? A FRAGMENTED
PUZZLE—I CANNOT FIT THE PARTS.

SELF-PORTRAIT: GUILT. © FRANCES MURRAY.

I DON'T KNOW WHAT IT
IS TO BE COMFORTABLE.
TO FEEL CALMNESS.
ANXIETY SWELLS IN MY
BELLY, A MAJOR-LEAGUE
SPONGE SQUEEZING MY
ORGANS. IT FEELS LIKE A
BAD SCIENCE-FICTION
MOVIE EXCEPT IT'S MY LIFE.
I LAUGH. IF I DON'T, I'LL
CRY. I THINK ABOUT WOODY
ALLEN AND SHOULD FEEL
RELIEF, BUT I DON'T.
IT'S NOT FUNNY BEING
NEUROTIC EXCEPT WHEN
YOU'RE WATCHING IT.

SELF-PORTRAIT: DISTRESS. © FRANCES MURRAY.

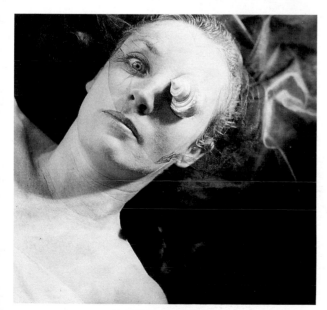

SELF-PORTRAIT: DESIRE. © FRANCES MURRAY.

Exercises for Right Brain/Left Brain Integration

FINE-TUNING NONLITERAL VISION

ONCE AGAIN, YOU SHOULD DO all of the exercises in this section in both black and white and color. As suggested in the first exercise for tapping into the right brain, scatter photographs on a large surface and in various directions. Since you've done this before, shifting your point of view this way shouldn't be too difficult. However, in this exercise, once you've established the single unified image out of all of the photographs assembled, you must manipulate the pictures further to clarify what you see.

Although you'll be using the left brain's gift for directing the reconstruction, you might not be able to easily rationalize your choices. Don't worry. Some photographers go as far as to rebuild the subject in one of the individual photographs by using all of the other pictures on the table. The rebuilding can be as fanciful or as literal as you please. You might even take photographs of your home and build another "house" out of them as some people do with a deck of cards.

When I made a composite picture of a bridge, I photographed the individual images under the guidance of my right brain's interest in abstract fragments. At the same time, my left brain found the most effective way to convey the right hemisphere's sensitivity to the subject's rhythmic gracefulness along with a verbal message (below).

When I saw the photographs of the bridge fragments scattered on my worktable, the rhythmic flow of their juxtaposition all but jumped off the cutting board. However, that didn't seem to be enough for what I wanted in the picture. When I moved around another stack of pictures from a totally separate shoot, the "hotel"

pulled all of the fragments together for me. It addressed the coldness of the snow and everything a bridge stands for to me— a point of transition, a place where nobody stays except temporarily on their way somewhere else.

❧

ANOTHER WAY TO IMPROVE your nonliteral vision is to combine pictures that weren't originally intended to be combined. Mark Feldstein assembled a group of right-brain-inspired images that he initially shot separately (opposite). The final photograph is a result of a holistic, right-brain sense of formality united by an intellectual deduction.

There is a sensuality to the pig's head and grapes. I like the going in and out of the vine and its relationship to the railing in the top picture and the curb. The pig's head was on the street. The picture is in black and white, so you can't see that the darkness at the base of the head is not shadow but blood. A man happened to walk up to the pig's head, and I photographed his foot. But I didn't know if his foot would be in focus because of the camera that I was using. I also didn't know how it would play. It ended up, in fact, giving scale to the pig's head.

The top image works as a dream. There are many antithetical angles in this combination. The shadows and vines feed the continuity. The pig's eye is like one of the grapes. I like the ambiguity of the sensuality of the grapes and the disgusting pig's head with the stamp of the Food and Drug Administration. I chose the top peaceful picture to escape the conflict between the blood and the grapes.

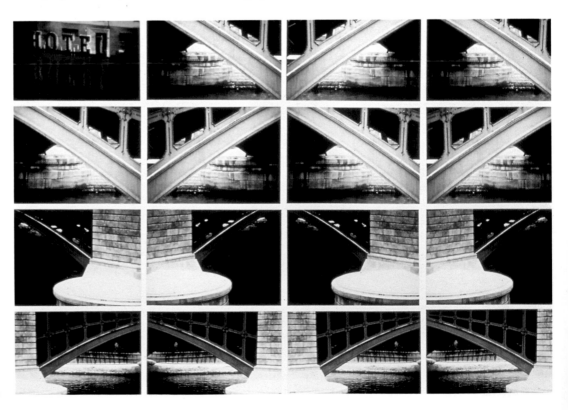

© KATHRYN MARX.

PIG'S HEAD.
© MARK FELDSTEIN.

WHILE FELDSTEIN FOUND new dimensions by juxtaposing various single images, Andreas Mahl altered an original picture by juxtaposing it with itself. He'd already experimented with this process and thought about the possibilities before applying it to this particular photograph. Nevertheless, he met with a few unexpected yet positive results. Then Mahl permitted his intuition to lead him in different directions, such as working horizontally (below).

I started this piece with a traditional, classic black-and-white photograph of a nude. After the photograph was printed slightly out of focus to highlight the reflections on the soft patina of the skin, I put two photographs together. The first time I did this was for an exhibition on the manipulation of photographs. I was looking for something new, and I did this with flowers and a self-portrait.

I found that when I did this with the body, it gave another architecture to the body, another dimension. I have also done this in vertical. But with this picture, I worked horizontally because it was more harmonious with the lighter and darker areas of this particular photograph. I found that when the forms are more convex and concave, it is more effective when it is horizontal. The vertical cutting can cut the lines which are already vertical. Therefore, they would not be seen as well.

I am not intellectual, but most of my work I do think out before. I never manipulate a photograph because it is not good. I simply look to take the photograph further. I look at the photograph and choose what to do so that I can take it and myself further.

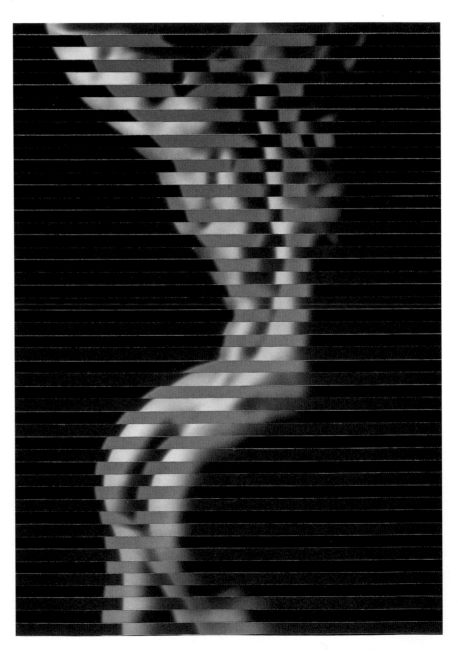

NU, NOIR ET BLANC.
© ANDREAS MAHL.

EXCHANGING BLACK AND WHITE AND COLOR

FIRST, TAKE A PHOTOGRAPH in black and white or in color. Make it either literal or abstract, and in sharp or soft focus. The second shot you take will be the opposite. So, if the first photograph is soft-focus, color, abstract image, the second photograph will be a sharp-focus, black-and-white literal interpretation. Beatrice Delrieu, for example, began with a black-and-white photograph and interpreted the nuances in color (below). This photograph of a precise detail shows the great potential of her imaginative and metaphorical right-brain impulses.

When I painted the piece at the left, it was according to the colors that I saw in the density of the black-and-white photograph. I see the orange, blue, and green. That is the composition of color, and the shape simply followed what I wanted to show of the square. All of the essential elements are shown within. All of the rest is within the free drawing of the surrounding black and white. The black-and-white photograph is to the right because it is lighter. The paper is light, white. The painting is on thick papier-mâché.

SQUARE NO. 3 (40 × 70CM). © BEATRICE DELRIEU.

DOCUMENTING AN EVENT WITH A SINGLE IMAGE AND A SERIES

FOR THIS EXERCISE, YOU must take a series of photographs that reveal the progression of an event. However, when you're shooting these images in successive order, you must wait until your instincts tell you that it is the right moment to make the photographs rather than your eye-clock or any other kind of external prompt. At some point during the event, shoot a single photograph that describes the event as well as the sequence. This sole photograph should be representative of both the event and your feelings about what you've seen.

When viewers look at the images, they should get a clear idea of what the basic reason for the event was. They should also get a first-hand sense of what it was actually like. So let your sensitivity create a photograph that portrays the feelings of the participants, including yourself, as well as any tension that existed. Claude Alexandre shows how both a single, all-inclusive image and a series of images can successfully capture an event.

This series is a segment of a ceremony. It is the preparation for a ritual. Her eyes are closed, in fact, as she isolates herself with a sort of meditation. In the first photograph, the makeup has been partially applied. In the second photograph, the makeup has been completed. The woman lets herself go in the third shot.

I photographed the hand before thinking that I should have a picture of her hand to symbolically fulfill the series of the ceremony. In the final photograph, she is waiting for the ritual to begin (a suspended moment).

I am a witness "objective," (although objectivity does not exist). I do not interfere with what is happening, like a reporter. I stay with my impulses vis-à-vis which moment I choose to take the photograph. I feel that I am on the exterior and choose what moment to enter and then leave.

I prefer not to think. If I think, I lose the strength and spontaneity of my work. I work by instinct, although I first choose the events that I want to photograph. I shot the first two photographs from the back because I felt, after walking around her, that this was the point of view to take. Everything said so, the light, the fact that she was sleeping.

In the single picture from the ceremony, we see the same mystery in the eyes, the makeup is completed, but now there are tears. The tears say that the event has already happened; the preparation is in the past. It is in profile because of the light on the tears, and the details are so well outlined on her face. We see the reality from behind the makeup, but the mystery stays whole because we do not know what happened or why, and it is, in fact, of no importance. This becomes simply a conflict between life and death.

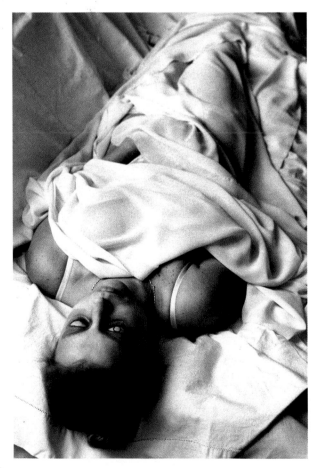

PHOTOGRAPHS
© CLAUDE
ALEXANDRE.

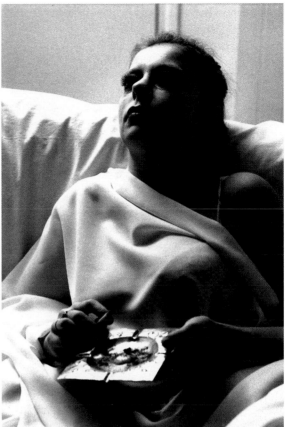
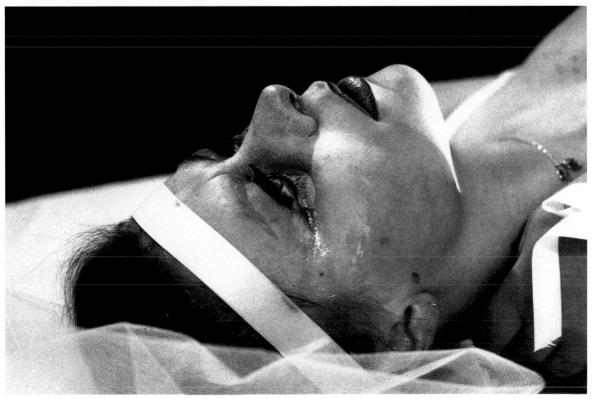

DOCUMENTING AN EVENT WITH PHOTOGRAPHS IN SEQUENTIAL ORDER

HERE, THE FIRST STEP IS to shoot an event, such as a parade, a ceremony, or a softball game. Next, take the resulting photographs and create an arrangement that conveys the experience as precisely as possible. The individual detail photographs can be interpretive in content or form, but they must be placed in strict successive order. Suppose, for example, that you decide to document a crowd being ushered out of a train station because of a fire. You may want to record some of the passengers' fear or panic by capturing facial expressions on film or by literally burning the edges of the

final prints. Just make sure that the relationship between these frozen emotions and the sequence of specific incidents is clear.

Aram Dervent used this approach in order to record the progress of women's pregnancies. Following a strict successive schedule, he began documenting each pregnancy one week into the fourth month and ended two weeks into the eighth month. Although the exposition of the progress is historically precise, half of the 250 images are, in fact, the ordinarily discarded side of a Polaroid picture. The project culminated in left-brain convergence.

Who is to say which side of the Polaroid film is the most valuable, that the negative is of no use? Together, they are an entity. Polaroid paper, when it is separated, the two pieces of paper create one photograph.

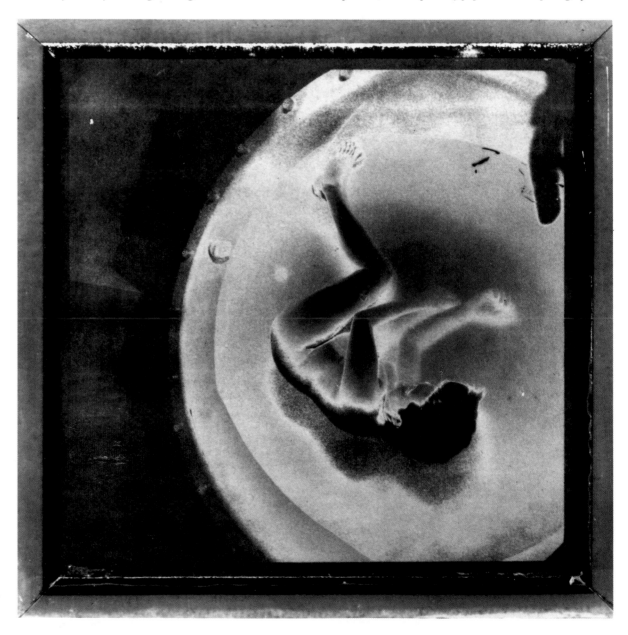

METAMORPHOSE,
1988–1992.
8 MOIS, 2 SEMAINE.
PHOTOGRAPHS
© ARAM DERVENT.

The values placed on what is waste and what is worth using is instituted by society. People say, "This is good; this is bad." I free myself by using both sides of the Polaroid. After all, reality is merely what we bring to the photograph. The negative is constructed by the positive, and the positive side in the negative. In fact, certain negatives are richer than the positives, the conventional banal image.

When I took these photographs, I knew that I would be using both sides. But this had nothing to do with how I took the picture. The image, in fact, does not interest me as much as it is the support for me to go further. There is an image which sleeps within the photograph taken the way the child is inside the mother.

In the exhibition, the negative was placed to the left because technically it becomes the positive. The photograph was taken from my skylight above my bathtub because I wanted a photograph of her in the water. I took 125 photographs in this series, so there were 250 photographs in the exhibition. I had an exhibition of every photograph taken from the fourth month of the woman's pregnancy unless the pictures were absolutely unreadable. The idea of choosing "aesthetically" which photographs to show is to go by a word which is used by society as their idea of beauty, which they wish to enforce on the world. I wanted to clearly document the period of a pregnancy. Every one-hour session was shown, from the fourth month and one week until the eighth month and two weeks.

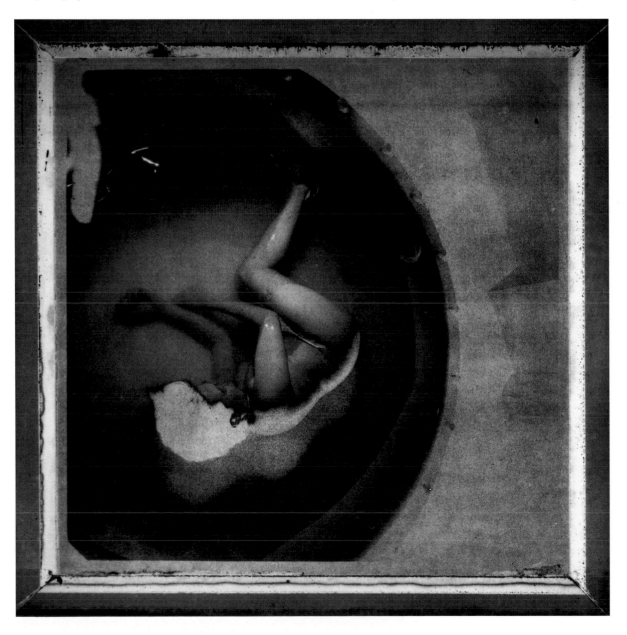

DEFINING AN ABSTRACTION

GIVE A VERBAL DEFINITION to an abstract photograph. In other words, use words. The verbal addition should be a definitive, clear-cut lead to the meaning of the image so that viewers can readily understand it. Be sure to use an abstract photograph taken from a subjective, imaginative point of view. You'll then see how such a picture can be enhanced or clarified by an explicit guide for viewers, who are often willing to have their interpretive thoughts dictated or manipulated. Nancy Wilson Pajíc describes the method she uses to create integrated images (below).

A great way to get out of my own preconceptions is to use "found" images. I have one pile of contact sheets and one pile of images which I have collected from various places, such as magazines and newspapers. My photographs with text are usually taken spontaneously, and then the mechanism of juxtaposition with text comes into play. The taking of pictures is often the most banal part of my creative process. The resulting image often serves merely as raw material.

I am a firm believer in photographic accidents. Instead of throwing away something, try different ways to recuperate "failed prints." The failed print is the one you can afford to try the craziest things with and, thus, the one which eventually leads to progress. I am juxtaposing phrases and pictures, making a lot of trials, and letting things happen until something "sticks."

ભ

PHOTOGRAPHS LIKE PAJIC'S, in which the text and image aren't conceptualized together beforehand, exemplify left- and right-brain integration. After the photographs are taken from the right-brain impetus, the left brain associates a deductive message and merges the two elements to create one imaginative photograph. Give it a try.

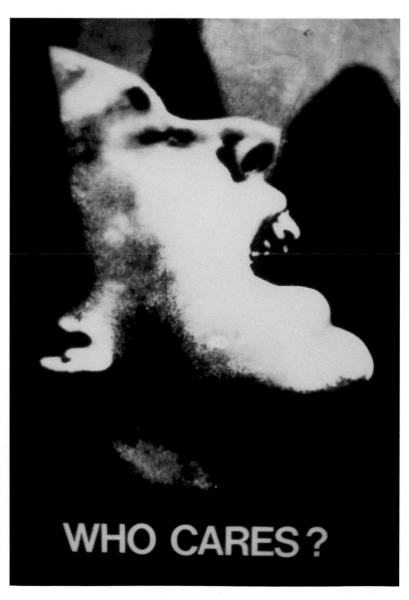

© NANCY
WILSON PAJIC.

WHO CARES?

MIXING THE ABSTRACT AND THE PRECISE

THE GOAL OF THIS EXERCISE is to shoot precise details of an experience, place, or person, and then to transform the pictures into something abstract. In retrospect, feelings are usually involved. These sentiments will be your guide during the transformation.

First, take the highly literal photographs and then make them reflect either the feeling that the subject evoked in you, the feeling of the subject, or the feeling you had during the actual experience. The possible results are seemingly endless. You might work with the negatives rather than the prints themselves, frame the central image with some of the prints, sandwich two slides together, or impulsively choose details, thereby increasing the number of options. I decided to mix the abstract with the precise when I came across a fairly common tree in St. Tropez (below). By placing the slide face to face with itself, I was able to reveal another aspect of my experience of the place.

This photograph is composed of a tree trunk in St. Tropez, a detail of the place transformed into a detail of the feelings I had while staying in the place. I sandwiched two identical images together in such a way that the mirror image of this physical detail became established in the realm of the obscure fantastic. It is the vaguely cloaked obscene, the colors of the tree bark as well as flesh.

KATHRYN MARX.

TRANSFORMING THE LITERAL INTO ITS METAPHOR

HERE, YOUR GOAL IS TO TAKE a photograph that is a straightforward picture of your subject. Using your imagination, you then increase the accuracy of the photograph by exploring your own vision of the physical detail. The goal here is not to render the original image unrecognizable, but to make it even more precise. The reasoning behind your style and your emphasis of a particular detail may be intuitive, but the final image should be a readable enhancement of the original. In essence, you deliberately manipulate the image into a metaphorical image of itself. Bob Bishop utilized this approach to more accurately reveal his feelings about his subject, which the first shot he made was unable to do (below).

With the machine I was able to take this photograph to where I wanted it to be. The computer has opened up possibilities and new potentials for me. When I saw the hands with the stones, I wanted a painterly feeling. The hands were carrying the earth next to the belly as if carrying life. I saw the painting in my mind. The hands were very important, but not in their given quality. However, with the computer, I was able to give the hands their importance, the texture I saw before taking the photograph. I manipulated the image until the rocks no longer had the look of stone, but a greater roundness so that they almost looked like eggs.

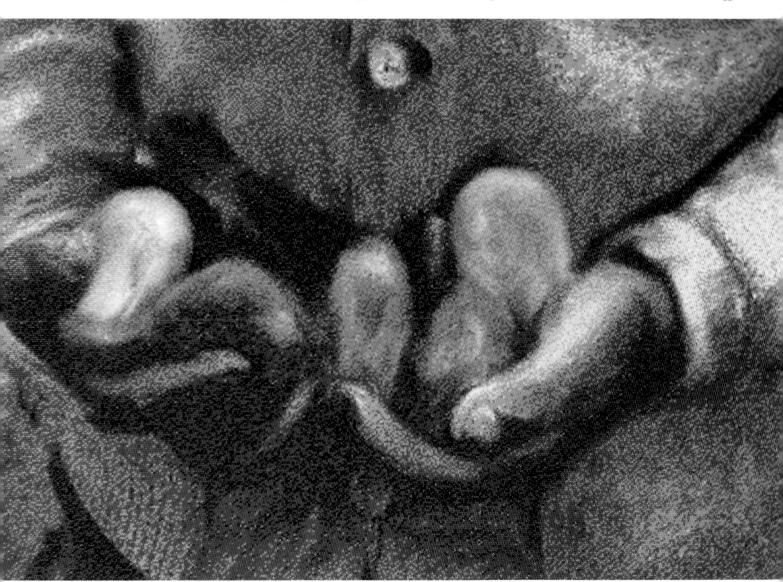

ROCKS IN HANDS. © BOB BISHOP.

IN ORDER TO TRANSFORM AN IMAGE, Pierre Cordier decided to utilize text as the physical object (below). For him, the picture of the words is more important than the words' metaphorical meaning. Although the result was also a chemigram of Cordier's personal interior, the final image is a decisive enhancement of Borges's poem.

This chemigram is inspired by a poem by Jorge Luis Borges, "La Suma," 90 words, 406 letters, in Spanish. I read Borges for years. I did not make this chemigram in order that the viewer could actually read the poem. It is, in fact, the spirit of Borges as much as it is mine. For me, the visual counts more than the meaning or symbolism within. Most important is the visual image rather than its significance. I do want people to see the text, but not necessarily be able to read word for word what is in it.

This chemigram is about one of Borges's dreams. He was "reading inextricable texts in which the words become confused, where everything becomes a labyrinth of letters." I was in a sort of labyrinth myself at the time that I did this work. So this piece is a chemigram from the interior, an image of the interior. I was working on myself as much as this work by Borges.

Letters, for me, are abstract. The letter A, for example, does not exist. It is, in fact, an abstraction as soon as it is transposed. Borges's poem, as a chemigram, is the poem without its contents, yet the poem is a chemigram because of them.

CHEMIGRAM 15/9/91. FROM "LA SUMA" BY JORGE LUIS BORGES. © PIERRE CORDIER.

LA SUMA

A MAN PLANS TO DRAW THE WORLD. THE YEARS PASS: HE FILLS A SURFACE WITH PICTURES OF PROVINCES, KINGDOMS, MOUNTAINS, GULFS, SHIPS, ISLANDS, FISH, HOUSES, INSTRUMENTS, STARS, HORSES, PEOPLE. JUST BEFORE HIS DEATH, HE DISCOVERS THAT THIS PATIENT LABYRINTH OF LINES TRACES THE IMAGE OF HIS OWN FACE.

JORGE LUIS BORGES

PHOTOGRAPHING PORTRAITS

FOR THIS EXERCISE, YOU MUST shoot a series of photographs detailing your subject. This person can be yourself or someone else. The details in each image should capture the essence of your subject; this is critical. Each portrait should be able to stand alone. The next step is to combine the individual pictures in a way that you feel best reveals your subject's personality. For example, you might want to place the image of a broad smile next to that of a frown if the subject is moody. You might also decide to arrange the shots so that they describe the person's physical features rather than emotional state.

During a rapid shooting session with photographer Andreas Feininger, my impulsive, intuitive side guided me. My left brain helped to determine which pieces were necessary or expendable in terms of making the portrait informative (right). Ultimately, however, my right brain completed the order of the vital images.

This portrait of Andreas Feininger was taken with two rolls of film in less than 10 minutes. I didn't plan to photograph his hands, but his ease with his surroundings of nature, home, and wife seemed suddenly exemplified in his hands.

Then I saw Feininger's way of shooting nature when I focused on those hands with my zoom lens. I couldn't pull it away once I saw the magnificent texture of his skin—the same pull I imagined he must feel when he is shooting one of his incredible spider webs. Composing the portrait, I added his profile to show the sharpness, the precision of his angular face which corresponded to the precision of his black-and-white work of the New York skylines and reportage. I deleted as many images as possible until I said to myself, "That's just enough."

❧

MARIANA COOK'S PORTRAITS also speak of a strong integration of her left- and right-brain tendencies (opposite). While she uses the subtle, abstract qualities of black-and-white film, this film is her tool of precision. Although the shoot proceeds from an intuitive point of view, the pictures render her subjects unmistakably identifiable.

I photograph in black and white because it is by definition an abstraction from reality. I like that. I miss the texture of paint in color photographs. I love paintings, and I love black-and-white photographs when they are rendered with beautiful tonal qualities.

My work is mostly intuitive. I rarely know very much about my subjects. For example, I have photographed a lot of writers but almost never read their books. On the other hand, the good print craft comes from a conscious knowledge. I am able to emphasize the expressive subtleties through my use of craft.

© KATHRYN MARX.

CARLOS FUENTES AND HIS DAUGHTER. © 1992 MARIANA COOK.

PHOTOGRAPHING ARCHITECTURE

HERE, YOUR TASK IS to document the building or tearing down of a structure. Your photographs should either reveal literal details of the structure or convey an abstract sense of it. You may want to add text to the abstract photographs that either document what you've witnessed or further describe the building. You may want to build the literal photographs into multiple or layered images.

An alternative is to add a video, other photographs, or materials that have nothing to do with the literal subject, but that enhance the sense of what you felt when you witnessed the construction or destruction of the architecture. You may also present a series of abstract detail photographs that, by virtue of their arrangement, concretely define the subject. Tom Drahos explains how he built and then photographed an entire installation (below). He explains that his installations have no precise approach. However, his intellectual interrogation of the subject's reality guides the overall composition. Drahos's goal, to address such questions, serves to stimulate further questioning and discussion among viewers.

I work with film and photographs, as I am becoming more and more interested with the philosophical relationship between images and reality, and beyond this with the very nature of images being merely a reflection of reality. In my installations of constructions, I believe that I show that there is something sacrificial about the metamorphosis images impose on reality. And this is perhaps the grounds of any creation.

What is reality? The reality of an image or of a city or of the relationship of the three? My installations do not have an objective character. It is a process, a system of open signs, the meanings of which cannot be separated from its public. I am only a mediator. I can go past the traditional categories of painting, photography, and film by working with my installations which have no specific approach, but which develop organically. In fact, it is this interaction of mediums which opens the perspective to the spectator. A reportage of 4,000 photographs would not suffice. I push my photographs past their limits. I try to preserve the possibilities of fiction by denying the photographs the basic characteristics of photography.

COURTESY OF THE GALERIE BOUQUERET + LEBON, PARIS. © TOM DRAHOS.

LIKE ALL OTHER SUBJECTS, architecture can stimulate the involvement of both the left and right brain. When Dominique Gaessler photographed haystacks, his holistic right brain guided the overall composition, while his left brain determined the vertical perspective (right and overleaf). The placement of the haystacks' details provides a clear sensation of their texture and architectural power. Ultimately, his feeling for his subject dictated the split second when he pressed the shutter-release button.

I photographed the haystacks vertically because the haystacks are a monumental kind of architecture. Every year, they are a different form, but always functional. They cannot be placed elsewhere nor otherwise. They are stacked to last and take up the least amount of space. They are also arranged so that when it rains, the water cannot pass through and spoil the hay. The haystacks do not last very long, but do return every year. It is an architecture which punctuates the countryside, specific to this one place in France (Seine et marne).

Each ball of hay (or squard) is like the bricks of a house. Each holds each other up, like bricks. They are closer at the bottom than at the top. If it falls, the hay is spoiled. It is like a monument in that it is so compact that the water cannot get in. The rigorous construction is at the same time quite fragile since it is made of hay. However, together it is solid and sure. The line is in the middle of the photograph with respect to the object, also acknowledging the fracture. They are, in their right, perfect objects.

Behind the haystack is an architect, the farmer. But what interests me is the form. There is a mystery within, imposing and sensual. There is a balance of the form, and the line is close enough to the center to show its symmetry.

When you shoot with a 4 × 5 camera, you are sure of your shot. All of the pictures in this series were previsualized. I returned to the same place after going there several times for the right light. Although it was all previsualized, it was also intuitive at the same time. The meeting between me and this subject was quite fortuitous. It was a matter of respect for what was before the eyes. I wanted to share my emotion of falling in love with these haystacks. There was a contrast of intentions, so there was no one approach. But the dominant desire was to give others the emotion that I felt, however with the strategy of documentation.

I studied the area, its aesthetics. I did not think at all when I saw the hollows from certain angles. It was a fraction of a second when I saw it and photographed it. It was an obsession, these haystacks. I fell in love with the form, and I wanted to give and do my best for the object, my love, and myself.

MEULES DE PAILLE. © DOMINIQUE GAESSLER.

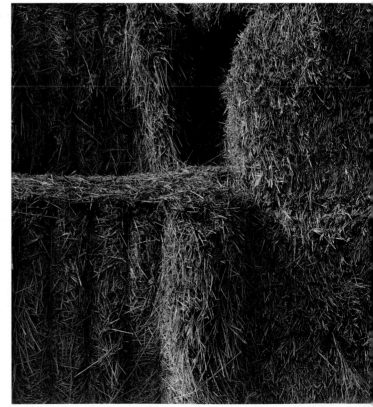

MEULES DE PAILLE. PHOTOGRAPHS © DOMINIQUE GAESSLER.

THE MOST STRAIGHTFORWARD, literal approach to an unusual structure can involve the imaginative impetus of the right brain. My photograph of this house is the result of this type of combination (below).

When I saw this house on the island of Bonaire, I first noticed the lavish canal system cut into the barren land around it; there was a distinct absence of trees or brush of any kind. It wasn't until after much closer scrutiny that I noticed that the chateau was missing its roof. The only way to capture this stark absurdity was to shoot the house in an absolutely straightforward manner. This also matched my first reaction to the place; there was something peculiar about it without knowing precisely what it was.

© KATHRYN MARX.

EXPERIMENTING WITH PROCESSES

HERE, YOU SHOULD TRY various calculated, technical techniques with your most abstract photographs. Use methods that have prescribed results, such as treating prints with chemicals in the darkroom. In this way, you'll be tapping the resources of your right brain for the initial abstract image and then applying your left brain's technical dexterity.

The most important aspect of this exercise is having an intellectually determined goal in mind. You must know why you want to treat an image in a particular way. For example, what do you wish to say by retouching your picture with a specific chemical combination? At the same time, however, you must be open to potentially making what are commonly—and sometimes unnecessarily—called mistakes. You may even discover a whole new process of post-shooting manipulation. Jerry Uelsmann explains the advantages this open-minded approach offers, as well as how your images may benefit from it (below).

My images are constructed in the darkroom. I cater a lot to accidents. I work with what I call "photosynthesis," based on perception and progress. As I tried out different combinations—in much the same way that I work in the darkroom when I am manipulating various negatives—meaningful comparisons emerged. Most of these comparisons had to do with different treatments of recurring elements or themes sometimes used many years apart.

Some of my psychologically motivated photographs seem to express the darker side of myself; others seem to embrace the Jungian notion of human consciousness. It always comes back to the fact that it is important for me to create images that challenge one's sense of reality. The darkroom experience affords us the opportunity for new beginnings.

© JERRY N. UELSMANN, GAINESVILLE, FLORIDA.

WITH A TREMENDOUS AMOUNT of technical knowledge, Nancy Wilson Pajic is not only open to "accidents" in the darkroom, she attempts to create situations in which surprises are likely to take place. Her images reflect her willingness to experiment (below).

> I am always in the process of inventing ways of circumventing my implacable logic and opening up my horizons. Deciding to abandon painting and to work with photography was one such way to ensure that unpredictable effects and accidents produce results that exceed or escape my preconceptions. As I got better at exposing film and printing photographs, the accidents got fewer and farther between. So I began to invent other tactics to create surprises for myself, to stimulate my own imagination and hopefully the imagination of those who look at what I have done.
>
> In this photograph, I first used a plastic pocket camera, the equivalent of a Donald Duck camera. The camera took 110 film and produced a bad negative. Then I used a developing process which exploited the faults in the negative. Then by making the print bigger, I further exploited the bad quality by getting a lot of grain in the print. But it was so extreme, the effect ended up being that of pointillism. At that time, I was working on a series of subtitled images. This picture ultimately looked like the end of a movie; thus, I added the text "FIN."

ↁ

PAJIC'S USE OF THE 110 pocket camera was a logical choice for producing imprecise material to inspire her imaginative potential. The abstract nature of the clouds becomes the pictorial definition of the word "fin," or end. The word cancels any conjecture on the viewers' part regarding the metaphorical implication of the clouds. They don't imply heaven, rain, or God. Pajic narrowed the image's original right-brain abstraction through the process of convergence. The result is an example of left-brain absoluteness.

The impulse to exploit what most people would think of as bad is one of the gifts of the right brain. It enables you to go beyond rational prejudgments and to let your instincts be your guide.

After completing this group of exercises, you'll have a strong sense of how the right and left hemispheres of the brain can work together to form a single image or series. Your abstractions will, perhaps, have found their most effective means of clarification, and your strongly directed photographs will have discovered a new avenue of spontaneous release.

I hope that my left-brain goal for this book has been realized. Because everyone has stronger right- or left-brain tendencies, I want to help you make effective choices. For those of you who are so rationally directed that the idea of photographing music is unthinkable, I hope that you are now open to this illogical possibility, or at the very least are willing to redefine your concept of logic. In much the same way, I hope that those of you who photograph only the invisible have discovered new concrete ways to communicate your "visions" to others.

It is my deepest wish that the insights of the photographers included in this book have brought you closer to what you see, how you feel about it, and how to show it most effectively. My left brain hopes that all of you have found this book to be a new, practical inlet into your brain's enormous amount of untapped potential. My right brain just gets excited at this prospect.

FIN OVER PROMENADE, 1988. FROM THE "OPEN ENDINGS" SERIES. © NANCY WILSON PAJIC.

INDEX